Global City Futures

Global City Futures

DESIRE AND DEVELOPMENT IN SINGAPORE

NATALIE OSWIN

THE UNIVERSITY OF GEORGIA PRESS
Athens

Portions of this work appeared previously in the following publications: Chapter 2 appeared in an abbreviated form in 2010 as "Sexual Tensions in Modernizing Singapore: The Postcolonial and the Intimate," *Environment and Planning D: Society and Space* 28(1): 128–141. Portions of chapters 1 and 3 appeared in 2012 as "The Queer Time of Creative Urbanism: Family, Futurity and Global City Singapore," *Environment and Planning A* 44(7): 1624–1640. Portions of chapters 2 and 3 appeared in 2010 as "The Modern Model Family at Home in Singapore: A Queer Geography," *Transactions of the Institute of British Geographers* 35(2): 256–268. Parts of the introduction appeared in 2015 as "World, City, Queer: The Sexual Politics of Global Urbanism," *Antipode: A Radical Journal of Geography* 47(3): 557–565.

Most University of Georgia Press titles are
available from popular e-book vendors.

Printed digitally

Library of Congress Cataloging-in-Publication Data

Names: Oswin, Natalie, 1971– author.
Title: Global city futures : desire and development in Singapore / Natalie Oswin.
Description: Athens [Georgia] : The University of Georgia Press, 2019. | Series:
    Geographies of justice and social transformation ; 44 | Includes bibliographical
    references and index.
Identifiers: LCCN 2018042682| ISBN 9780820355016 (hard cover ; alk. paper) |
    ISBN 9780820355023 (pbk. ; alk. paper) | ISBN 9780820355009 (ebook)
Subjects: LCSH: Gays—Singapore—Social conditions—20th century. | Gays—
    Singapore—Social conditions—21st century. | Homosexuality—Political
    aspects—Singapore. | Gay rights—Singapore. | Singapore—Politics and
    government—1965–1990. | Singapore—Politics and government—1990– |
    Economic development—Political aspects—Singapore.
Classification: LCC HQ76.3.S55 O89 2019 | DDC 338.95957—dc23
    LC record available at https://lccn.loc.gov/2018042682

CONTENTS

FIGURES

ACKNOWLEDGMENTS

This book about the politics of heteronormativity in Singapore has taken much longer to write than I initially anticipated it would, in part because finding a balance between the "productive" and "socially reproductive" sides of my life has been difficult over the last several years. I know I am far from alone here, among people like myself whose reproductive desires are sanctioned by the state in which they reside and especially among those who due to homophobia, transphobia, racism, sexism, national bias, and more are not in such a position of privilege. Creating familial lifeworlds can be a joyous and rewarding process. But it can also be difficult and consuming, especially when state and society put up barriers for those cast as less than "desirable" as primary caregivers for future generations. I raise this point because it resonates so strongly with the book's concerns, and because it is one that is too often unacknowledged in the field of academic knowledge production. What's more, it is unacknowledged by design. The divisions between public/private, productive/reproductive, male/female, straight/queer, cisgender/trans, "savage"/civilized, traditional/modern have been well deconstructed through decades of postcolonial, critical race, feminist, trans, and queer scholarship. But these binaries persist in all kinds of ways in all kinds of contexts, with profound material effects.

While this project's completion was delayed as I embraced caregiving responsibilities, it was also delayed as I grappled with how to convey my argument. I have been terribly conscious that the kind of expansive queer critique I advocate for in this book's pages is largely absent within urban studies and Singapore studies (and many other fields of enquiry), not because many brilliant scholars somehow happen to have a collective blind spot, but because systems of production everywhere, including systems of knowledge production everywhere, have long been buoyed by inequities and injustices tied to the sort of majoritarian heterosexual reproductive futurisms I critique in this book. Along the way, I wrote drafts upon drafts of all its chapters, trying to find ways to interest a broad audience in thinking about urban and national development through the lens of LGBT issues, and trying to find a voice and a tone that would be heard. In the end, it may be that my aim to find a wide audience, even among critical scholars, is no more than a pipe dream. Though I purposefully did not put the word "queer" in this book's title, it is in the book's description. And even if it were not there, the book's main emphasis on the politics of majoritarian heterosexual reproductive futurism may keep many of the readers I want to speak to away from it. For, despite my assertions to the contrary in the book's description and throughout its pages, many not-so-critical and even critical scholars will see it as a book about "minority" issues rather than a book about socioeconomic development and urban futures, and they simply will not see the former as central to the latter. So, I first thank the readers of this book. I hope it in some small way contributes to thinking about how we can critically approach the task of building just urban futures.

More broadly, colleagues and friends at several institutions have provided encouragement and collegiality over many years. As a doctoral student at the University of British Columbia in the early 2000s, when the field of "queer geographies" was not nearly as established as it is today, I found mentors in Nick Blomley, Derek Gregory, Jennifer Hyndman, Geraldine Pratt, and Juanita Sundberg, and a fellow traveler in my then grad student colleague Eric Olund. I still greatly value their early support. At the National University of Singapore, where I was first an overseas student interloper, and then a postdoctoral fellow and assistant professor, I thank a wonderful community of scholars, students, and friends, including Noor Abdul Rahman, Tim Bunnell, TC Chang, Arianne Gaetano, Daniel Goh, Elaine Ho, Philip Holden, Shirlena Huang, Lily Kong, Lisa Law, Lin Weiqiang, Loh Kah Seng, Anant Maringanti, Pow Choon-Piew, Kamalini Ramdas, Shen Hsui Hua, James Sidaway, Tracey Skelton, Monica Smith, Teo You Yenn, Woon Chih Yuan, Brenda Yeoh, and Henry Yeung.

At McGill University, my academic home since 2008, Sebastien Breau, Ben Forest, Kevin Manaugh, Sarah Moser, Raja Sengupta, Renee Sieber, and Sarah Turner make the Department of Geography a collegial and rewarding place to work. Sarah Turner also deserves special thanks for doing close readings of many drafts of chapters in this book, and for always pushing me to write clearly. The McGill Institute for Gender, Sexuality and Feminist Studies does extraordinary work with far too few resources and recognition, and I am profoundly grateful for the work that director Alanna Thain, past director Carrie Rentschler, and faculty and faculty affiliates Bobby Benedicto, Mary Bunch, Jenny Burman, Michelle Cho, Gabriella Coleman, Jonathan Sterne, Jeremy Tai, Ipek Tureli, and many more do to foster queer, trans, feminist, critical race, and postcolonial scholarship and activism on our campus. At McGill, I have also been fortunate to learn from and with junior scholars including Ali Bhagat, Noelani Eidse, Gilly Hartal, Tai Jacob, Spencer Nelson, Rae Rosenberg, Kai Kenttamaa Squires, and the students who have enrolled in my Sex, Race, and Space and Queer Geographies courses over the years.

The ideas in this book have also been shaped by my engagements with scholars and friends in geography, urban studies, and queer studies whose work I admire, and with those who kindly engaged with my work in various ways. I thank

Peter Adey, Ben Anderson, Anjali Arondekar, Alison Bain, Gavin Brown, Michael Brown, Kath Browne, John Paul Catungal, Sharad Chari, Rosemary Collard, Nicole Constable, Deborah Cowen, Debanuj Dasgupta, Jessica Dempsey, Kate Derickson, Robert Diaz, Petra Doan, the late Glen Elder, Kathryn Furlong, Jack Gieseking, Kevin Gould, Ju Hui Judy Han, Chris Harker, Phil Hubbard, Jan Simon Hutta, Tariq Jazeel, Larry Knopp, Travis Kong, Eithne Luibhéid, Martin Manalansan, Lauren Martin, Patricia Martin, Eugene McCann, Will McKeithen, Beverley Mullings, Amber Musser, Catherine Nash, Heidi Nast, Shiri Pasternak, Linda Peake, Norma Rantisi, Farhang Rouhani, Ted Rutland, David Seitz, Rashad Shabazz, Svati Shah, Mimi Sheller, Mary Thomas, Alex Vasudevan, Eleanor Wilkinson, and Audrey Yue.

At the University of Georgia Press, I thank Mick Gusinde-Duffy for his interest in and patience with this manuscript over many years, Nik Heynen for his support before he left the series' editorial team, and especially Mat Coleman for picking up the project and carrying it over the finish line. The anonymous reviewers provided much to work with in their comments on a previous draft of the manuscript, and I owe them a big debt of gratitude for helping me see how to reorganize the argument at a crucial stage.

Finally, Cher Campbell and I met at Bar Code (which is sadly no more) on Toronto's College Street in late 1999. Today, after many moves and travels and ups and downs, she is still my home, along with our two fierce, wonderful daughters Jenna and Vanessa. These three mean the world to me, and I dedicate this book to them.

Global City Futures

INTRODUCTION

The small Southeast Asian island nation of Singapore punches well above its weight on the global stage. It attracts considerable scholarly, policy, and popular attention and is a key nodal point in the global economy, and a wide range of urban and national governments look to it for "best practices." Its extraordinary and extraordinarily rapid socioeconomic development and efficient, largely corruption-free government since it became an independent city-state in 1965 yield much admiration. But Singapore also attracts much critique, as its polity is dominated by one party that governs from the top down, curbs civil liberties, curtails access to public space, and limits public discourse. Furthermore, its economy today is more polarized and is managed with less emphasis on minimizing wealth inequalities than at any prior time in its postcolonial history. In short, while the dominant discourse positions the city-state as an urban leader, many commentators raise important concerns about the developmental path it takes. In this book, I contribute to critical understandings of the city-state and to questioning of its desirability as a model for urban futures everywhere. I challenge the limits the Singapore state places on its population's desires and futures and advance a queer critique of global urbanism.

On May 16, 2009, an estimated twenty-five hundred people gathered in Singapore's Hong Lim Park to participate in Pink Dot, the city-state's first ever large public assembly of LGBT (lesbian, gay, bisexual and trans) Singaporeans and their supporters. The atmosphere was upbeat and celebratory. There were a few short speeches. But mainly the crowd, clad in pink as requested by organizers, casually socialized until it was assembled into a large circle photographed from the roof of a nearby building. The event was a milestone. Until the late 1990s, police raids of cruising grounds, closures of LGBT bars and saunas, and suppression of media and artistic expressions of LGBT experiences through censorship were common in Singapore. But by 2009, the city-state's social, political, and economic landscape had changed in ways that allowed events like Pink Dot to occur.

In the decades after it became a sovereign city-state in 1965, Singapore experienced astounding socioeconomic growth, earning a reputation as an "Asian Tiger" by the mid-1980s. Yet the People's Action Party (PAP) government, which has ruled Singapore uninterrupted throughout its postcolonial period, has never taken for granted its position at the front of the global city pack. The PAP forcefully and frequently exhorts Singapore's populace to adopt an ethos of adaptation and change to facilitate continued progress, sustained development, and a bright future. Discursive efforts to propel Singapore and Singaporeans forward, with assurances that the future will be a bright one if the citizenry cooperates, and with warnings that the end is nigh if it does not, reached an especially fevered pitch in the 2000s. For instance, still-current prime minister Lee Hisen Loong made the following statement in 2005 on the city-state's fortieth national day: "What will Singapore be like forty years from now? I can't tell you. Nobody can. But I can tell you it must be a totally different Singapore because if it is the same Singapore as it is today, we're dead. We will be irrelevant, marginalised, the world will be different. You may want to be the same, but you can't be the same. Therefore, we have to remake Singapore—our economy, our education system, our mindsets, our city."[1] Going back to 2003, then prime minister Goh Chok Tong succinctly conveyed the same sentiment: "If you can't evolve, big as you are or prosperous as you may be, you die like the dinosaurs" (quoted in Elegant 2003).

To remain competitive in the global economy, in the late 1990s Singapore's government fundamentally altered its economic development plans and began to transform its manufacturing-based economy into a knowledge-based/creative economy. By the early 2000s, the PAP recognized that the authoritarian image that the city-state had projected since independence was a hindrance to its economic transformation. As urban policy advisors increasingly counselled at that time, the highly skilled workers who purportedly fuel creative economies want personal freedoms and a certain "buzz" in the cities in which they choose to settle. In one of its many efforts to shed images of a heavy-handed government and a sterile cityscape, the Singapore government shifted its official stance on LGBT issues from outright condemnation to limited tolerance. As a result, police raids of cruising grounds ceased, LGBT commercial establishments were allowed to operate largely unhindered, and censorship restrictions were slightly loosened. Legal and policy change to counter discrimination against LGBT persons did not follow, however. Thus the need for Pink Dot, which still forms annually in this creative city as "a symbol of Singapore's more inclusive future."[2] Year after year, the event attracts large crowds and corporate sponsors as well as sustained local and global media attention. The existence of Pink Dot and other LGBT advocacy and community organizations in the city-state is wonderful and important. As Lynette Chua notes in her excellent book-length account of the ways in which local LGBT activists pragmatically respond to an illiberal sexual politics, "to speak out is to mount the first act of resistance" in Singapore (2015, 5). Pink Dot speaks out to work toward a future Singapore "in which all Singaporeans are free to love and be loved."[3] It speaks out to work toward the broadening of the definition of Singapore's national family.

I attended Pink Dot in 2009 as someone who, like LGBT Singaporeans, falls outside Singapore's national family. I am a Canadian citizen and have maintained residency in Canada since mid-2008. In May 2009, I was in Singapore to continue research that I started while I lived in the city-state from 2002 to 2008. From 2002 to 2005, I was a trailing spouse. My partner was one of the throngs of "foreign talent"—the Singapore state's loaded term for "skilled" migrant workers— welcomed in the 2000s as part of the push to build a knowledge-based/creative economy. While my partner had an employment pass and the state grants dependent passes to the spouses of "foreign talent," I could not procure one since these passes are given to opposite-sex married couples only. I therefore entered the city-state on one-month "visitor" passes, which I could string together as I had the means to leave and reenter the country frequently enough to renew them. With my PhD in hand in 2005 and an academic position secured at the National University of Singapore, I then joined the ranks of the "foreign talent" population, a member of which I remained until we departed Singapore in 2008. We left for many reasons, but especially for one. Though my partner applied for and was granted permanent resident status while we were there, and thus we did not need to worry about her immigration status should she lose her job, we wanted to become parents and could not do so in the city-state. In Singapore, same-sex couples are barred from adoption services, and it is illegal to provide assisted reproductive technology services to single and/or lesbian women. Uncomfortable with available options to skirt the state's regulations, like seeking in vitro fertilization services in neighboring countries with different legal frameworks or establishing separate residences so that one of us could pursue adoption as an apparently "single" person, we chose instead to return to Canada to build our family.

We had strong friendship and professional networks in the city-state and wanted to continue our lives there while—as the Singapore government asks of the "foreign talent" to whom it offers the option of naturalization—contributing to the shaping of the city-state's future. It was therefore difficult for us to choose to relocate. But we had the choice. At Pink Dot in 2009, I thought about the many people in Singapore who do not have options to pursue such relatively easy paths to full citizenship and reproductive futures. I thought of those Singaporean LGBT persons who do not have the means, job prospects, or freedom from local dependent and caregiving responsibilities to resettle elsewhere. I also thought of the many temporary migrant laborers—or, in the again loaded parlance of the Singapore government, "foreign workers"—in the city-state. This population toils largely in the domestic service, construction, and retail sectors. Like the "foreign talent" population, its numbers swelled throughout the 2000s, part of the same economic shift that brought my partner and me to the place at that time.[4] But people who enter Singapore under the "foreign worker" category, unlike their "foreign talent" counterparts, do not have the option of becoming naturalized in the city-state. Furthermore, these migrants cannot bring family members with them as dependents to Singapore. Nor can they marry or have children while on a worker's permit. As such, "foreign workers" share with both LGBT Singaporeans and LGBT "foreign talent" the experience of being positioned outside Singapore's national family and excluded from full participation in its bright global city future.

As we formed the Pink Dot, I thought specifically of the weekly assemblies of temporary migrant laborers who are a part of Singapore's urban landscape. Those workers with a day off on weekends generally leave their dormitories or employers' homes and eke out space in which to commune with fellow migrants in public spaces.[5] The gatherings of those who converge on the Little India neighborhood are large and highly visible, while countless small groups of friends and coworkers meet less obviously in parks, at shopping centers, and in other public areas throughout the island. These gatherings are comparable to Pink Dot in that they are formed as attempts to create community and belonging in the absence of secure family ties. They also differ in key ways. Migrant worker gatherings in the city-state are weekly rather than annual, and informal rather than centrally organized. They are also cast as personal rather than explicitly political, and they do not garner media fanfare or corporate sponsorship.

These two kinds of gatherings, and the LGBT and foreign worker advocacy movements in Singapore more broadly, are never linked in local public discourse. Indeed, links between migrant and LGBT lives are rarely made in urban policy or scholarship anywhere, as the former tend to be cast as products of sexual and gender politics, the latter as products of race, class, and gender politics. Yet a diverse body of queer scholarship shows that these two issues and movements, along with others, ought to be considered together. For sexual minority and gender identity experiences and discriminations are not single issues that can be fully understood and challenged by considering and interrogating homosexual-heterosexual and transgender-cisgender binaries alone. Rather, moving out from LGBT politics, many scholars and activists have shed light on the broader politics of "heteronormativity," the geographically and historically specific coincidence of race, class, gender, and sexual norms that reaches far beyond sexual and gender-identity struggles to shape familial and intimate relationships, domestic norms, migration flows, national identities, and more. They call attention, in other words, to the crucial but far too often overlooked question within urban studies of who gets to fully participate in the production and social reproduction of our world's cities. As José Muñoz powerfully notes, there is "no future but the here and now of . . . everyday life" for many when "the only futurity promised is that of reproductive majoritarian heterosexuality, the spectacle of the state refurbishing its ranks through overt and subsidized acts of reproduction" (2009, 22).

In this book, I argue for the need to situate the LGBT issues that have recently gained prominence in Singapore within a wide field of power relations. I consider the "gay issue" that has been in the local spotlight for some years now and go further to analyze the city-state as a hetero*normative* space. Against the overwhelming tendency within both urban studies and Singapore studies to treat sexual and gender identity politics as issues of relevance only to constituencies of sexual and gender minorities, I respond to homophobia and transphobia and critique the broader race-, class-, gender-, and sexuality-based politics of heteronormativity of which these ills are part. I thus advance a queer reading of Singapore that sheds light on the lives of "queers" and much more. That is, I advance a reading of the city-state that interrogates its government's stubborn resistance to policy and legislative change that would foster LGBT equality, while calling attention to the ways in which many more than LGBT persons are "queered" and cast as mere supplements in the global city. Visions of just urban futures, I argue here, must include analysis of and challenges to the fraught politics of reproductive futurism within which LGBTs and many other "others" are caught up.

Global City, Singapore

On its first annual National Day in 1966, the late Lee Kuan Yew—Singapore's prime minister from 1959 until 1990 and then a senior government official through 2011—declared, "Singapore can set the pace . . . [by demonstrating] that we are a forward-looking, not a backward-looking society, not looking to the past for examples of patterns of behaviour and conduct completely irrelevant in the modern society that we now find ourselves . . . but that we have the forward, the inquiring outlook, and are keen to learn, keen to make a success of the future" (Lee 1966). Throughout the city-state's postcolonial period, the PAP that Lee helped found has governed uninterrupted and in a relentlessly future-oriented manner, always striving to be economically competitive and a leading global city. Countless economic development and urban concept plans have produced near constant upward growth in this corner of Southeast Asia, and Singapore's government has exhibited the "forward outlook" of which Lee spoke while translating the desire for "success" into socioeconomic development that is nothing short of extraordinary. Singapore's transition from "third world to first" over the initial decades of its postcolonial period has received a great deal of attention from scholars and policy makers alike (for instance, see Huff

1995; Olds and Yeung 2004; Perry, Kong, and Yeoh 1997).[6] Equally widely known and admired are the efforts its government has undertaken since the late 1990s to turn its manufacturing-based economy into a new knowledge-based economy (Kong 2000; Sparke et al. 2004; Wong and Bunnell 2006; Yeoh and Chang 2001). As Tim Bunnell notes, there is by now "no shortage of cities, especially in Asia, wishing to do a Singapore" (2015, 1991). Various city and national governors around the world actively attempt to emulate its urban, housing, transport, education, migration, and economic policies and practices.[7]

The dominant Singapore story is thus a success story, and the city-state's developmental trajectory is the envy of urban governments everywhere. It has certainly achieved global city status according to the scholarly definition of the term. The notion of the "global" or "world" city concertedly entered Anglo-American urban studies with the publication of Peter Hall's (1966) *The World Cities*. In that text, he observes that "there are certain cities [i.e., world cities] in which a quite disproportionate part of the world's most important business is conducted." His focus is on the growth trends and planning issues facing such cities rather than on fleshing out this new city "type," however, leaving in-depth theorization of the notion to others. John Friedmann's (1986, 71) "The World City Hypothesis" takes up this task. He argues that "key cities throughout the world are used by global capital as 'basing points' in the spatial organization and articulation of production and markets," and begins to think about such cities as a group by setting out characteristics they purportedly share and arguing that they constitute a global urban system that is hierarchically arranged. In addition, Saskia Sassen's (1991) pivotal *The Global City: New York, London, Tokyo* develops the notion that "global cities" are command and control centers in the global economy. Against the argument popular at the time of that text's publication that globalization would spell the end of geography, she examines the three cities listed in the book's title in detail to show that while space-shrinking technologies enable a dispersal of economic activities, that dispersal also creates a huge demand for expanded central control and management functions. "Global cities," she argues, meet that demand and function as key nodal points in the globalized economy, as sites where extraordinary flows of capital, labor, and technology come together. Finally, the Globalization and World Cities Study Group and Network (GaWC), created in 1998 by Peter Taylor and Jon Beaverstock, emerged to further understandings of both individual global cities and their connections and interactions. Among its core contributions, the GaWC developed a data matrix composed of headquarter and subsidiary locations of leading accountancy, advertising, banking and finance, insurance, law, and management consultancy firms across the globe, and used these data to categorize and rank cities as part of a "world city network."

These influential contributions in turn inspired the growth of a huge related literature, and the notion of the global city as a command and control center of the global economy is now a powerful one for scholars and urban practitioners alike. University-based research groups pump out rankings of global cities and study their economic growth potential and connections,[8] and urban governments everywhere strive to attain or maintain reputations as global cities by attracting the higher order service sector activities that yield the greatest value in the contemporary international economy. Global city status is viewed as desirable by many urban actors, and efforts to attain it shape urban futures everywhere. But the idea of the global city, in scholarship and practice, is not without detractors. Many scholars question the usefulness of the notion as defined above, arguing that the literature's narrow focus on cities as nodes in the global economy results in scholarship that in fact tells us very little about the complex relationships between globalization and urbanization. That is, many scholars point out that biases toward economism and categorization in mainstream conceptualizations of the global city lead to the neglect of the social and cultural dimensions of urban-global relationships. Critics also challenge an overemphasis on categorization and a preoccupation with identifying a hierarchical global urban system within the literature (see, for instance, Gugler 2004; Keil, Wekerle, and Bell 1996; Robinson 2002). Brenda Yeoh cuts to the heart of these critical assessments with her statement that "the global city concept is often used not so much as an analytical tool but as a 'status' yardstick to measure cities in terms of their global economic linkages, to locate their place in a hierarchy of nested cities and to assess their potential to join the superleague" (1999, 608).

These critiques have spawned a healthy counter-literature. Critical urbanists push us to think about cities as *globalizing* rather than *global*. They argue for the analytical benefits and social justice imperatives of moving from a focus on categorization to a focus on process and for the vital need to extend the globalization-urbanization research nexus beyond the constricting focus on determining which cities are world cities. They push us to interrogate the global city as postcolonial (King 1991), glocalized (Brenner 1998), transnational (Smith 2001), or ordinary (Robinson 2006), for instance. Furthermore, initiatives to image cities as "global" have come under fire from critical scholars and other observers for their bureaucratic, hierarchical, competitive, rational, and socially polarizing tendencies (for example, Bunnell 1999; Ghertner 2015; Kanna 2011; McCann 2004).

Such concerns resonate with the Singapore case. While the city-state's government strives constantly to stay ahead of the pack and at the forefront of the global economy, it often chooses to "stay behind" on social issues. As current PM Lee states,

> When it comes to issues like the economy, technology, education, we better stay ahead of the game, watch where people are moving and adapt faster than others,

ahead of the curve, leading the pack. And when necessary in such issues, we will move even if the issue is unpopular or controversial. . . . On issues of moral values with consequences to the wider society, first we should also decide what is right for ourselves. . . . So, we will let others take the lead, we will stay one step behind the front line of change. (Lee 2007)

Singapore's population is compelled to constantly adapt and change for the sake of the economy, while far-reaching social control measures curb and contain Singapore society in all kinds of ways, with often socially unjust results. Social policy, like urban development, is conceived and implemented from the top down in Singapore, and the city's present and possible futures are shaped by official desires to remain globally competitive rather than by the aspirations and inspirations of its diverse populace. As such, narratives that cast Singapore as a model city are challenged by critical voices within media, policy, and scholarly circles. Compelling analyses point out rising income inequalities (Chang, Huang, and Savage 2004), the lack of a social safety net (Asher and Nandy 2008; Jones 2012), gender biases that place the burden of social reproduction on women (Teo 2016, 2011; Yeoh and Willis 2005), a profoundly unjust migrant labor regime (Poon 2009; Yea 2015), significant restrictions on civil liberties (George 2000), and more (Chua 2012; Tan 2007b). They call out, in other words, the ways in which colonizing, nationalist, elitist, and patriarchal tendencies strongly shape life in the city-state. Early iterations of such critiques were made bravely, and often at considerable personal cost as the PAP government has historically dealt harshly with detractors.[9] In contemporary Singapore, the discursive field is somewhat more open since the current government recognizes that authoritarian curbs on public discourse do not foster a creative city feel. While Singapore is still governed with a strong hand and considerable limits on public discourse and participation remain in place, alternative visions at least now have some air.

This book breathes in this counternarrative space. With many others, I am troubled by the fact that in Singapore, a city with a high quality of life for most of its inhabitants and one that so many other governments seek to emulate as a model, poverty, exclusion, and marginalization persist for many. I am troubled that this city-state with a government so concerned with ensuring its bright future, and with such demonstrated capacities to build one, limits the potential of various groups to participate in public life. The existing critical literature on global city Singapore calls out social injustices in the city-state. But, sexual and gender identity politics go largely unmentioned in this work on Singapore and in studies of global urbanism more broadly, to the detriment of both literatures. The global city, I argue, ought to be critically read as colonizing, nationalist, elitist, patriarchal, *and* heteronormative.

Global City, Queer

"Queer" is a complex term that signals two predominant meanings. While it is now used most widely as a simple descriptor for LGBT communities and social movements in many places, its deployments in activist and scholarly circles have grown out of specific lineages and meanings (for an excellent overview of queer theory's emergence and key tenets, see Jagose 1996). For many decades in Anglo-American locales, the term "queer" was generally used as a derogatory, slang term for non-heterosexuals. But certain radical HIV/AIDS organizations began to reappropriate it in these same locales in the early 1990s. As groups like ACT UP and Queer Nation fought against the stigma of the widespread labeling of HIV/AIDS as a "gay disease," they advanced a radical, sex-positive, and antiassimilationist politics that they labeled "queer" rather than "gay and lesbian." By reappropriating the term, these organizations rejected its negative connotations and thereby challenged the notion that there is any "normal" sexuality. In this usage, a queer identity and politics "embraced literally anyone who refused to play by the rules of heteropatriarchy" (Bell and Valentine 1995, 21).

At around the same time, and mostly within the same contexts, queer entered the academy as a new mode of theorizing. Here too the term took on a radical, politically confrontational tone. Queer theory, as it emerged within literary theory circles in the 1990s, asserts that sexual identities are social constructions that do not preexist their worldly—that is, cultural and linguistic—deployments. It maintains a focus on the plight of sexual minorities while fundamentally challenging the empirical validity and conceptual usefulness of identity categories. As Fran Martin (2003, 25) states, "As 1990s feminist theory did with 'women' and postcolonial theory did with 'race' and 'culture,' queer theory was concerned to disrupt the assumed universality and internal coherence of previous categories of identification in 'gay and lesbian identity.'" The insight that sexualities are performed, that they are something we *do* rather than something we *have*, has formed the basis for the development of a now highly significant interdisciplinary and international literature. By acknowledging both hegemonic heterosexuality and marginal sexual and gender identities as socially, historically, and geographically contingent, work within queer studies has taken on the critical tasks of understanding the ways in which sexual identities are performed and of challenging the myriad processes through which sexual norms become naturalized in a wide range of times and places. Queer theory is, in other words, a poststructural theoretical approach that challenges the presumed fixity of sexual and gender identities and critiques the ways in which sexual and gender norms are deployed as part of broad structures of governance.

This work has made the extremely important contribution of putting the lives of LGBT people on the agenda for scholars across the humanities and social sciences. It has at the same time offered a powerful critique of the notions of sexual and gender identity. Moving away from essentialist, a priori understandings of sexuality and gender, queer theory attends, as legal scholar Janet Halley succinctly notes, not to "who we are but how we are thought" (2000, 67). It pushes us to understand homophobia, transphobia, and heterosexism—and indeed all modes of sexual and gender regulation—in the context of broad sets of power relations. As such, much queer scholarship productively eschews a proper object (see Butler 1994). This is a crucial point. Queer theory, though it emerged in good measure out of the urgent need to validate and protect the lives of those cast as sexual and gender minorities, offers an epistemological approach that challenges the notion of identity itself. It offers a non-identarian framework, and therefore begs for the advancement of a subjectless critique. Otherwise put, while queer theory has been an important vehicle through which LGBT experiences have gained critical academic attention, it pushes us to go beyond this literal referent. It pushes us, as Cathy Cohen influentially argued in 1997, to move away from the fallacy that the tensions animating sexual and gender identity politics can be explained by a heterosexual-homosexual binary alone. Heterosexuality and heteronormativity are not synonymous, since "identities of race, class, and/or gender either enhance or mute the marginalization of queers, on the one hand, and the power of heterosexuals, on the other" (Cohen 1997, 447).

An interdisciplinary body of queer studies work builds on this insight that heteronormativity is not reducible to heterosexism by dissecting "the ways in which discourses of sexuality are inextricable from prior and continuing histories of colonialism, nationalism, racism, and migration" (Gopinath 2005, 3; see also Eng, with Halberstam and Muñoz 2005). Neoliberalism and desire (Rofel, 2007), gendered diasporic subjectivity (Gopinath 2005), transnational migration regimes (Luibhéid 2013; Shah 2012), and biopolitics and terrorism (Puar 2007) are just some of the topics that have been scrutinized by scholars who innovatively put queer theory into conversation with postcolonial, critical race, feminist, and other critical theories to understand the workings of heteronormativity in an array of contexts. This work goes beyond examinations of sexual and gender identity politics per se to explore the ways in which heteronormativity works as a major defining cultural force that is entwined everywhere with other defining cultural forces such as capitalism, patriarchy, and racism/ethnic bias. As such, there is now a large body of scholarship that demonstrates Michael Warner's point that queer "rejects a minoritizing logic of toleration or simple political interest-representation in favor of a more thorough resistance to regimes of the normal" (1993, xxvi) and challenges us to reckon with the fact "that sexuality isn't always or only about sexuality, that it is not an autonomous dimension of experience" (1995, 368). Very much of this work, it is crucial to note, embraces the label "queer of colour critique." Work in this vein specifically puts queer theory in conversation with postcolonial theory, woman of color feminist thought, critical race theory, critical ethnic studies, and Indigenous studies and importantly pushes for an intersectional sexuality studies geared toward building coalitions across modes of difference (see, for example, Bacchetta, El-Tayeb, and Haritaworn 2015; Driskill et al. 2011; Ferguson 2004; Muñoz 1999; Snorton 2017).

In terms of the relationship between queer studies and urban studies, cities are of course important locales in which sexual and gender norms play out; and queer scholarly investigations of queer politics, subcultures, and individual experiences in cities abound. Cross-disciplinary studies of LGBT lives in western cities (and suburbs) have been plentiful over the last few decades within queer studies (for instance, see Abraham 2009; Bailey 2013; Chauncey 1994; Chisholm 2004; Delaney 1999; D'Emilio 1983; Hanhardt 2013; Houlbrook 2005; Manalansan 2005, 2003; Rushbrook 2002; Tongson 2011) and various studies of LGBT politics in nonwestern cities have emerged more recently (for instance, see Benedicto 2014; Engebretsen 2014; Jackson 2011; Kanai 2015; Manalansan 2015; Merabet 2014; Stout 2015; Tang 2011; Tucker 2009). Queer scholarship that examines the urban dimensions of hetero*normativity* is lacking, though, and this book seeks to address this absence.

To clarify, I am not saying that recognition of heteronormativity as a multivalent force with implications for gendered, racialized, classed, and sexualized subjects is lacking within queer work that focuses on cities. On the contrary. Much of the work mentioned above utilizes queer approaches that are inseparable from postcolonial, feminist, and critical race approaches. Thus, the challenges of racism, sexism, classism, as well as homophobia and transphobia for queer and trans individuals and communities are very well interrogated. For instance, Martin Manalansan's important book *Global Divas* (2003) examines the global and transnational dimensions of gay identity as lived by Filipino immigrants in New York City. He insists that many queers of color create alternative paths to queer modernity and citizenship, in and through global cities, and thus challenges the implicit whiteness of much western queer thought. His subsequent article "Race, violence, and neoliberal spatial politics in the global city" (2005) is another important reference point. In that piece, he "critically examines and documents the violent remapping of lives, bodies, and desires of queers of color in contemporary New York caused by neoliberal practices" and details how "homonormativity creates violent struggles around urban space by queers of color" and thus brings questions of race, ethnicity, immigration, and diaspora centrally to the fore (2005, 142). Furthermore, Bobby Benedicto's *Under Bright Lights* (2014) sets out a creative reading of gay spaces in Manila that provocatively and productively attends to the problem of what he calls "third world queer complicities" with neoliberal logics. In *Queer Visibilities* (2009), Andrew Tucker examines Cape Town in the post-apartheid era and finds that as divisive apartheid legacies persist, there is no coherent "gay community." As such, he explores how "white," "coloured," and "black"—in the South African vernacular—gay men experience their queerness in the city very differently. In a final example, Noelle Stout's *After Love* (2015) highlights race, nationality, gender, and class differences in her ethnographic examination of the entanglements of lesbian and gay social networks, same-sex prostitution economies, and sex tourist circuits in Havana.

But while there is much work that considers the full range of heteronormativity's effects on queer communities and politics, there is little that considers heteronormativity as a force that shapes the lives of non-LGBT subjects. Scholarship that examines commercial sex in the city develops such a line of enquiry most fully. As Phil Hubbard notes, such a focus helps to clarify how heterosexual norms are reproduced spatially through the exclusion and containment of commercial sex work away from "family spaces" (2008, 646), and a wealth of historical and contemporary studies on sex work and urban red light districts make important contributions to our understanding of the relationship between sexuality and space (for instance, see Howell 2004; Hubbard 2004; Papayanis 2000; Pitman 2002; Shah 2014). Furthermore, Meredith Raimondo considers discourses surrounding the heterosexual transmission of AIDS in Belle Glade, Florida, and finds that "unlike constructions of AIDS that equated gay men with inevitable death, risk lay not within the category of heterosexuality itself but in particular perverse heterosexualities" (2005, 61). She argues that though the prevalence of heterosexual transmission means that AIDS can no longer be cast as a gay disease, racialized narratives that "queer" certain expressions of heterosexuality have recontained the threat by establishing distance between the "proper domesticity" of the "general population" and the "spoiled domesticity" of racialized ghettoes of migrant laborers. Nayan Shah similarly uses the term "to question the formation of exclusionary norms of respectable middle-class, heterosexual marriage" (2001, 13) in his historical examination of public health and Chinese immigration to San Francisco around the turn of the twentieth century. He argues that "the formation of respectable domesticity connected practices of individual health and sexuality to collective social well-being" (2001, 77). Given that not simply heterosexuals but white, middle-class, heterosexual couples with children were the societal standard, "Chinese bachelor sexuality is represented as deviant because the presumed sexual relations of these men living in San Francisco were considered nonreproductive and nonconjugal" (2001, 78; see also Briggs 2002).

In this book on Singapore's global city project, I extend understandings of the urban as heteronormative. There is much need for such an analysis given that there has been strikingly limited uptake of queer studies work within the broader field of urban studies. It is certainly well recognized within urban studies that cities play a profoundly important role in facilitating the formation of LGBT communities and movements around the world. It is also well recognized that LGBT issues are important urban issues. Indeed, most current texts on critical urban politics or urban social geography at least make mention of the relationship between LGBT subcultures and the city, and a smattering of articles on this same theme can be found in recent issues of urban studies journals (for instance, see Andersson 2015, 2011; Bell and Binnie 2004; Seitz 2015; Valentine and Skelton 2003; Waitt and Gorman-Murray 2011). In addition to the literature on LGBT lives and urban space (and particularly on "gay villages"), queer work has entered urban studies through Hubbard and others' work on marginal heterosexual sex work sites in the city. But as Hubbard states in his important book *Cities and Sexualities*, though it is well acknowledged that the city is a site of both sexual and gender possibility and regulation, many urban theorists do not acknowledge the importance of sexuality as "a vital dimension of social life—and one of the key factors that shapes our experience of the city" (2011, xv).

This fact is problematic. It is also, frankly, surprising. LGBT movements and issues have taken on truly global importance and reach in recent decades. Events like the passage of anti-gay laws in Russia ahead of the 2014 Sochi Olympics and the extension of the definition of marriage to include same-sex couples in Uruguay and New Zealand in 2013 have attracted worldwide media attention and debate. International and activist organizations such as the International Gay and Lesbian Human Rights Commission compile data on the legal status of LGBT persons in all the world's countries (see iglhrc.org for country reports and other documents), and since 2008, such information has been discussed by the United Nations General Assembly and has formed the basis of various nonbinding declarations (e.g., United Nations 2011). Furthermore, sexual difference is increasingly marshaled as a symbol of progress and modernity for the purposes of fostering national and urban competitiveness in various contexts, such as Singapore. That is, as NGOs and social justice groups in myriad national locales continue to strive for LGBT rights through largely urban-based movements, and as Richard Florida (2002) and other mainstream urban policy advisors popularly argue that successful cities within the global economy are ones that are "gay-friendly" (more on Florida in chapter 1), cities are more important terrains for sexual and gender identity struggles than ever before.

It is also surprising that queer studies has limited reach within urban studies given the extensive efforts in recent decades to diversify not only the field's topical coverage, but also its conceptual apparatus so that urban scholarship might better grapple with urban difference. Consider *Cities of Difference* (1998), the important collection edited by Jane M. Jacobs and Ruth Fincher. In their introductory chapter to the book, Jacobs and Fincher expound on the ways in which the "cultural turn" that swept through the social sciences in the 1990s profoundly changed how geographers and others understood identity in the city. Long-standing models (or "resilient" models as they describe them below) that understood differences such as race, class, gender, and sexuality as discrete identities that could be easily mapped and charted within urban space were unsettled by understandings of difference as mutually constituted, and by understandings of culture as always bound up with politics. Toward the chapter's end, they state, "These revisions have placed into question the frameworks by which we come to understand urban life and urban processes. 'The city' as an object of analysis has been irredeemably unsettled, and many of the more resilient ways urban processes are understood have been rendered problematic" (Jacobs and Fincher 1998, 2). Some years later, Jennifer Wolch wrote glowingly about urban studies as a healthily plural enterprise:

> In the journal *Urban Geography*, one can find articles on urban transformations around the world, feminist urban geography and queer theory, homelessness and welfare reform, urban identity and citizenship, racial segregation and environmental justice, patterns of e-commerce as well as traditional manufacturing, transportation and land use, urban governance regimes, implications of globalization and transnational immigration flows. The list goes on and on, speaking to the rich tapestry of the field as it has been woven throughout its recent history, nourished by the quantitative revolution, the rise of Marxian and humanistic geographies, and the effervescence of feminist, postmodern, and postcolonial thought. (2003, 645)

Today, even in the face of the undeniable rise and unprecedented reach of technocratic approaches to urbanism (for a description and important critique of such approaches, see Brenner 2013), the field of critical urban studies is alive and well. It has been particularly invigorated by a wave of postcolonial and comparative scholarship seeking to expand the field's geographical coverage and reorient it epistemologically (McCann, Roy, and Ward 2013; McFarlane 2008; Ong and Roy 2011; Robinson 2016; Roy 2014a, 2014b; Simone 2010). Whereas the mainstream of urban studies has historically been overwhelmingly western-centric, there is now, as Jennifer Robinson puts it, a "commitment to producing an understanding of the urban which is potentially open to the experiences of all cities," a new openness to "the world of cities" (2014, 57). To correct the consignment of nonwestern cities to the "waiting room of history," calls for the provincialization of western urban experiences abound. In response, there has been a proliferation of scholarship that, first, expands the very limited early mappings of "global cities" to recognize that cities like Singapore are central to the new economy and, second, examines the ways that all cities everywhere are transnational actors. Due to this cosmopolitan turn within urban studies, as Kate Derickson sums up, much work within urban studies now "draw[s] on postcolonial theory, subaltern studies, and feminist theory . . . as a political and epistemological strategy to refuse Eurocentrism and 'provincialize' urban theory that has been born out of observation of European and North American cities" (2015, 648). She further notes that work that seeks to world urban studies is work that seeks, "to locate political possibilities in emergent subjectivities and livelihood possibilities" (648), and that it productively recognizes "that there is not a singular 'urban story' to tell, other than that to insist that there are many urban stories" (651).

To thoroughly provincialize and decolonize urban studies, though, we also need to foster an urban studies that is open to the experiences of all urban dwellers, including those who are LGBT. I am not alone in making this point. Sophie Watson likewise notes the conspicuous lack of attention to sexual difference as urban studies has expanded its geographical reach, and problematizes this fact, asserting that "questions of gender, sexual and embodied difference are no less significant in the global south, and indeed arguably at this point possibly more so" (2014, 385). Furthermore, Jon Binnie, in an article on relational comparison within urban studies, suggests "that urban studies can be enriched by greater consideration of the role of desire, intimacy, and sexuality in practices of 'worlding cities'" (2014, 590; see also Brown 2008). We simply cannot fully understand the question "whose city is it?" (a question that underpins critical urban studies of all stripes—from work stemming from at least the 1990s onward on cities and difference, through the more recent worldings work) unless we interrogate urban experiences, development, and politics as imbued with sexual and gender identity politics and norms.

A postcolonial/worldly urban studies, as Roy argues, builds on the fact that "the periphery, even in its topological use, is an important conceptual device to decenter urban analysis," and even more significant "is the claim that the periphery is both a space in the making and a form of making theory" (2014a, 232). In a similar vein, Colin McFarlane argues that we ought to theorize from the "urban shadows," from the "spaces at the edges of urban theory" (2008, 341). He asserts that the periphery is theory, and by engaging with this paradoxical space, we might introduce a radical undecidability to the analyses of urbanism, and thus we might envision more just urban futures. In the contemporary scheme of things, LGBT subjects are certainly still out there in the periphery. For this reason alone, there is a need for a more concerted engagement between queer studies and urban studies. Beyond this need to put queer studies and urban studies into conversation so that urban scholarship can grapple with LGBT lives and social movements as pressing global urban issues, though, I also argue for the importance of bringing these fields together for the benefits that queer theory as a non-identarian approach might offer to urban studies. I argue not just for attention to the LGBT spaces and people of the city, but for the advancement of a queer approach to urban space.[10] I argue, in other words, for a queer approach that goes beyond the important but narrow focus on LGBT subjects and spaces in urban areas to consider the ways in which normative and nonnormative identities and practices construct and are constructed by urban development projects. In the chapters that follow, I approach Singapore as a city that is not just dominantly hetero*sexual* but fundamentally hetero*normative*. This approach brings into focus the ways in which intimate, familial, and domestic norms underlie the colonizing, elitist, nationalist, and patriarchal tendencies that existing critical scholarship already challenges in relation to this city-state. It brings into focus the importance of thinking about the politics of reproductive futurism when critically analyzing global city futures.

Queering Global City Singapore

As I discuss in chapter 2, some scholarship has emerged to champion LGBT rights in Singapore (e.g., Chua 2015; Yue and Zubillaga-Pow 2012), and mention of this aim is made every now and again in the broader critical literature. In this book, though, I argue for the need to take the perpetuation of sexual and gender norms much more seriously in analyses of cultural politics in this global city. From the starting point of the "gay" debates, the chapters that follow fan out to demonstrate that Singapore's developmental/global city project strands not just LGBT subjects in a state of arrested development. They show that, by design, the city-state's government's efforts to shape the public and private lives of Singapore citizens and residents in order to ensure perpetual forward movement and upward growth render many people across various modes of difference out of place and time.

In the face of activist and scholarly efforts to carve out a place within the city-state's landscape for sexual and gender minorities, the PAP has set firm boundaries, as noted above. While LGBT communities and subcultures have been allowed to expand and in many ways flourish since the early 2000s, legislative and policy changes to address systemic sexual- and gender-based discriminations and inequities have not occurred. As Prime Minister Lee Hsien Loong (2007) stated in response to activist efforts to repeal a colonial-era sodomy law, "there is space, and there are limits" (for more on this, see chapter 3). The government's justification for this stance, in short, is that "the family" must be protected. In response, in the chapters that follow I examine the "gay debates" and then turn the lens onto the family as an institution of the state, and particularly onto how governance in Singapore relies on a broadly consequential governance of intimate relationships. Specifically, I examine the ways in which a narrow notion of family became a key mode of social regulation through Singapore's late colonial and postcolonial periods to lay bare the well-entrenched truth that "the family" is a foundational element of Singapore's developmental project. I interrogate, in other words, the ways in which heteronormativity has been sedimented in the city-state for the sake of socioeconomic "development."

My queer critique of global city Singapore takes issue with the exclusion of LGBT people from full citizenship while also building a wide-ranging critique of what I identify (taking a cue from existing queer studies work) as an exclusionary politics of reproductive futurism in the city-state. I highlight the family's function as a regulative governing fiction and examine ways that a "proper family" has been carefully cultivated throughout Singapore's colonial and postcolonial history. The "proper Singapore family" plays a role in producing both a stable population of "quality" citizens as well as multiple "queered" others who fall outside the very particular heterosexual family norm upon which Singapore's developmental aims have come to rest. As such, the queer reading of the Singapore case that unfolds in the chapters that follow is of relevance to all those whose lives deviate from the norms of sexual, domestic, and familial propriety upon which Singapore's success has come to rely, and to those interested in rethinking the narrow notion of progress that has long guided the city-state's development. This queer reading shows that the heteronormative logic of urban and national development strategies in Singapore is tied in crucial ways to their broadly socially polarizing effects, and that existing emphases on the race, class, and gender dimensions of cultural politics in the global city are important but unduly partial.

Chapter 1 provides context for the rest of the chapters with a general overview of the socioeconomic development strategies that Singapore's government has pursued since Singapore became an independent city-state. It covers the export-oriented industrialization phase of the city-state's early postcolonial period, the subsequent regionalization drive, and the still ongoing pursuit of a knowledge-based/creative economy. The chapter highlights the fact that the PAP has positioned its citizenry as a key resource throughout its postcolonial history while expending extensive efforts to control that citizenry through massive social and spatial engineering projects and policies. Finally, it explains how its shifting approach to "culture" in its current creative economy phase has led to a liberalization of the polity, but one with such strong limits that no fundamental political change has yet resulted.

Chapter 2 begins to grapple with the confluence of intimate regulation and socioeconomic development strategies in Singapore by examining the debates over the place of homosexuality in the city-state that have raged since the PAP government began to liberalize its attitude toward sexual difference in the early 2000s in the context of its drive to foster a creative economy. While loosened restrictions on public expressions of homosexuality have allowed LGBT subcultures and activist/community organizations to flourish, the government has steadfastly kept enfranchisement off the table. In the face of this impasse, I explore why Singapore is still a "straight" space in this unprecedented time in its history of LGBT tolerance. Building on existing work on LGBT issues in Singapore, the chapter offers a reading of the always forward-looking Singapore government's willingness to "stay behind" on the issue of LGBT rights to point out that it seeks not to protect a narrowly hetero*sexual* norm but instead to protect a deeply foundational hetero*normative* logic. A close look at public discourse on homosexuality in the city-state shows that the government continues to marginalize sexual minorities not because they threaten heterosexuality per se, but because they threaten a specific family norm that is positioned at the center of Singapore society. Since this family norm is a mutual constitution based on race, class, gender, and nationality as well as sexuality, I argue for the need to move away from a narrow focus on an inclusionary sexual identity politics and toward the advancement of a more capacious critique of the politics of intimacy within Singapore's unjust citizenship regime.

Chapter 3 departs from the 2007 activist appeal for the repeal of Section 377A of Singapore's Penal Code, a colonial-era statute that prohibits "gross indecency" between two men. While the pro-repeal side argued that the statute is a colonial throwback that is out of place in contemporary Singapore, the PAP government responded that it is "part of our landscape" and opted to retain it (Lee 2007). However unwittingly, this assertion is not out of step with postcolonial theory's claim that the postcolonial condition is by no means beyond the colonial. The chapter takes this fact seriously and sets out a reading that excavates heteronormativity in Singapore as a colonial trace. Drawing on archival material from the late colonial period, it shows that while scant attention to homosexuality is found in the public record, the archives overflow with evidence of colonial efforts to produce a proper intimate sphere. Furthermore, the chapter demonstrates that these efforts to cultivate a respectable domesticity were animated by the colonial administration in concert with certain members of the colonized elite. It thus offers a history of sexuality that moves beyond identifying the origins of "gay" versus "straight" identity politics to illustrate the importance of considering the governance of intimacy in Singapore as a postcolonial phenomenon.

Moving out from the debates over the place of homosexuality in Singapore, chapter 4 focuses more specifically on the family norm that the PAP seeks to protect. Despite the Singapore government's success at entrenching a particular familial ideal as a norm within Singapore society, this strong state has not been able to instrumentally manipulate the reproductive preferences of its populace. Indeed, Singapore's fertility rate has been below replacement level since the 1980s, and this is a source of much official anxiety. While a dominant contemporary government narrative depicts the family as in crisis, critical commentators have responded with various policy solutions to this unusual inability of the strong Singapore state to manipulate its population. But this chapter shifts the focus away from the question of how these demographic "problems" might be overcome in order to take seriously this "failure" as evidence of the instability of the unit at the center of the hegemonic notions of appropriate intimacy. To consider exactly what sort of family the Singapore state is trying to shore up and why, it traces the ways that the PAP government picked up the late colonial interest in fostering the family form in earnest as part of its efforts to spur on Singapore's takeoff for modernization, and then carried this concern forward via a dizzying array of family planning, housing, and migration policies and more. The chapter moves out from the issue of LGBT exclusion/inclusion to account for a range of subjects—such as single mothers, members of the minority Malay community, and foreign workers—who are "queered" in postcolonial Singapore and to interrogate the heterosexual norm that underpins the city-state's developmental project as a source of both privilege and discipline.

The book concludes with a brief epilogue. Here, I pick up on the call for the "freedom to love" that unites the diverse groups composing Singapore's LGBT social movement. This phrase has so far been deployed to make demands for nondiscrimination toward LGBT persons and same-sex relationship recognition. But, as the book's chapters demonstrate, heterosexist legislation and policy remain in place not because of homophobia alone but because the establishment of intrusive modes of regulating intimate life within Singapore was in fact a key facet of the transition from colonial administration to postcolonial governance, and remains at the core of Singapore's global city project in ways that position many, many more than gays and lesbians as improper subjects. Since the politics of love are not merely identarian, the call for the freedom to love can and ought to be refashioned in ways that go beyond both the single issue and a politics of pragmatism, and we need to do much more than appeal for inclusion *along* the lines of race, class, gender, sexuality, and nationality. The book thus ends with a call to work *across* these lines by better merging the utopian impulses of critical urban studies, especially by decentering queer claims to and on space in the city-state to enable the centering of a much-needed project of decolonization.

Taken together, the chapters that follow build a critical analysis that identifies and questions the ways in which public life and intimate life commingle across multiple modes of difference in Singapore. Methodologically, my argument take shape as a genealogy built on readings of official and scholarly discourses rather than an ethnographic study of individual lived lives and experiences. As Julian Carter notes, following Foucault, a genealogical method is one that refuses "to explain history by reference to origins, causes, and inner truths; rather, genealogy traces the inherently political process by which some institutional and discursive effects get constituted as original, causative truths" (2005, 8). It foregrounds how individuals and groups are positioned in the world as the product-effects of discourse and practice, thus undermining efforts to pathologize difference while examining how notions of difference are shot through with power relations. The archival sources that I draw on come from the National Archives of Singapore, the National University of Singapore's Singapore-Malaysia collection, and the National Archives of the United Kingdom. Sources consulted include the records of government agencies such as the Housing Development Board and its colonial precursor the Singapore Improvement Trust, the Family Planning and Population Board and its colonial precursor the Family Planning Association, and the Department of Social Welfare; PAP government speeches since 1965; annual

Proceedings of the Legislative Assembly; daily newspapers such as the *Straits Times* and periodicals such as the *Straits Chinese Magazine* and *Utusan Melayu*; government housing and population policy publications; local social science books and theses on family, housing, and migration issues; correspondence between the Singapore colonial administration and the UK Colonial Office; and annual reports of the Straits Settlements. Contemporary sources include policy reports from and websites of government agencies and civil society organizations, contemporary print and local media, and secondary scholarly literatures.

Politically and conceptually, the chapters ahead ride the wave of the space-opening moment of creative urbanism in the city-state to advance readings of Singapore's archival and public record that make legible the emergence of various figures that fall outside logics of reproductive futurism. The overarching aim—to broaden discussions of progress and development in this global city so that notions of "success" might be recast and alternate possible urban and national futures might be envisioned—is a simple but potentially powerful one. As Judith Butler notes, while "one might wonder what use 'opening up possibilities' finally is . . . no one who has understood what it is to live in the social world as what is 'impossible,' illegible, unrealizable, unreal, and illegitimate is likely to pose that question" (Butler 1999, 7). Furthermore, following Muñoz, "the present is not enough. It is impoverished and toxic for queers and other people who do not feel the privilege of majoritarian belonging, normative tastes, and 'rational' expectations" (2009, 27). In global city Singapore, as everywhere else, the bounds of the possible and the violence of normative privileges require interrogation. A queer approach has much to offer to the critical project of re-envisioning global city futures.

CHAPTER 1

A Developmental City-State

In 1819, Sir Stamford Raffles established Singapore as a British trading port. By 1826, it was incorporated along with the ports of Penang and Malacca to form the Straits Settlements, which were administered by the British East India Company until their transformation into a Crown Colony in 1867. Direct colonial rule continued (apart from the 1942–1945 Japanese Occupation) until its formal end began in stages in the mid-1950s. Partial self-governance was attained in 1955, full self-governance followed in 1959, and Singapore joined the new nation of Malaysia in 1963. Prior to that union, the Singapore-based People's Action Party (PAP), led by Lee Kuan Yew, ruthlessly undermined local opposition forces and carefully forged ties with key Malaysian political actors under the assumption that a merger with Malaysia would secure a future for Chinese-dominated Singapore in a Malay/Muslim-dominated geopolitical region. This arrangement, however, did not last. Relations between the federal United Malays National Organization (UMNO) and the PAP rapidly and irreparably broke down. A difference in views on the way to deal with racial and ethnic difference within the new nation's political landscape was one of the main reasons why. In brief, the PAP pushed strongly for a "Malaysian Malaysia" built on a belief in meritocracy, while UMNO aimed to put in place affirmative action policies to deal with the considerable economic disparities that had developed between the Malay population and other groups—particularly the Chinese population—during the colonial era. On August 9, 1965, the Malaysian Parliament unanimously voted to expel Singapore from the nation. Lee Kuan Yew tearfully announced the separation at a press conference, an event since referred to in Singapore's historiography as "the moment of anguish" (Chua 2010, 338), and assumed the role of prime minister of independent, sovereign Singapore. Separation, for Lee, was "politically and personally traumatic" (Yao 2007).

The odds appeared stacked against a Chinese-dominated city-state located in this corner of Southeast Asia, and one with no significant natural resources to exploit aside from its location at the Singapore Strait and its resultant role as a key nodal point in global shipping routes. Yet, when British prime minister Harold Wilson wrote to express concern over the separation, Lee replied, "Do not worry about Singapore. My colleagues and I are sane, rational people even in our moments of anguish. . . . Our people have the will to fight and the stuff that makes for survival (quoted in Yao 2007, 2–3). Indeed, as Chua Beng Huat notes in relation to Singapore's early postcolonial years, under the leadership of Lee and his PAP government, "Singaporeans immediately ploughed into surviving the future with frenzy. Everything that stood in the way of economic development was removed without any sentimentality, as creative destruction necessitated by capitalist development" (Chua 2008, ix).

Since then, the PAP has relentlessly pursued economic development strategies in tandem with efforts aimed at urban renewal and population management while consistently creating a sense of urgency and crisis in order to maintain social order and "racial harmony." Its efforts, as mentioned in the introduction, have catapulted the city-state to the top of global city rankings and garnered it a far-flung reputation as a model city. Yet the contemporary PAP advises strongly against complacency. Cut to the words of current prime minister Lee Hsien Loong (Lee Kuan Yew's son) in 2015:

> We worry all the time. People say we are paranoid, which I suppose we are. And we need to be because, you know, at a higher level you expect to be at a higher level. You don't expect to go back to where you were in the 1960s. And yet it is not natural that we stay at this place. Is it to be expected that a population of three and a half million citizens and maybe a million foreign workers will have the best airline in the world, the best airport in the world, one of the busiest ports in the world, be a financial centre which is one of three or four key financial centres in the world, and an education and healthcare and housing system that gives us a per capita GDP which is—at least by World Bank calculations—higher than America or Australia or Japan? It is an entirely unnatural state of affairs and one which we should count our blessings for, if not every day at least every election.[1]

PM Lee spoke these words at "Singapore at 50: What Lies Ahead?," a conference put on by the National University of Singapore's Lee Kuan Yew School of Public Policy. The packed room of delegates laughed heartily at his punch line. Though delivered in a casual tone, his message was nonetheless serious. As countless PAP representatives have done numerous times over the last half century, PM Lee set out his party as the only viable option for continued success by commanding awe at its achievements. He stressed the need to stay the course with him and his government, to let them continue to set the agenda for the city-state and bring it to even greater heights. In doing so, he set out past from present, urging continual forward movement to avoid falling back.

In this chapter, I press pause on this neat progress narrative to provide a critical account of the ways in which the PAP government has repeatedly remade the postcolonial city-state of Singapore in ways that have achieved high levels of economic growth while fostering social control and claiming political legitimacy. Drawing on the large body of existing critical Singapore studies scholarship, I describe the key aspects of the PAP's efforts to shape and control Singapore society over its three major postcolonial phases of socioeconomic development—the export-oriented industrialization phase of the initial postcolonial period, the regionalization drive of the 1980s and early 1990s, and the current push to build a knowledge-based economy. I discuss top-down planning, attraction of foreign capital and technology, political dominance by a single party, economic growth coupled with resource distribution, mass depoliticization, significant limits on civil liberties, and extensive efforts to engineer urban space and citizenship as key characteristics of Singapore governance since 1965. To conclude, I highlight the growth of a sizeable critical literature that examines experiences of citizenship in contemporary Singapore from below, but that does so without analyzing the ways in which heteronormativity is a social force that actively shapes this global city project.

Becoming Singaporean

The first phase of Singapore's postcolonial socioeconomic development, covering the period from the mid-1960s to the late 1970s, is that of export-oriented industrialization. Thrust into its postcolonial era as a city-state with poor prospects for regional cooperation due to the failed merger with Malaysia, and without significant natural resources other than its sea-route locational advantage, the PAP set out to make global economic connections.[2] It was an opportune time to do so. The world market for manufactured goods was expanding as developed economies were experiencing relatively high growth rates and multinational corporations were diversifying the geographies of their production facilities in search of cheaper labor (Grice and Drakakis-Smith 1985). The PAP therefore worked to make Singapore an attractive place for capital to touch down by fundamentally remaking the city-state's social, political, and urban landscapes to create modern infrastructure, a population of dedicated and docile workers, and a stable political climate (Chua 1995). These were tall tasks as Singapore's tenuous geopolitical position was not the only difficulty the PAP faced in 1965. There were also formidable domestic challenges stemming from the colonial and transition periods as the PAP's grip on power was by no means locally unopposed at the time of Singapore's independence. In bringing the party to political prominence with the attainment of full self-rule in 1959, Lee Kuan Yew and his close associates turned on anticolonial actors such as worker and union movements, ethnic and clan associations, and communists and other leftists—indeed, repressively so, relying on tactics such as criminal charges leading to prison terms,

FIGURE 1.1. Statue of Stamford Raffles against the backdrop of Singapore's contemporary central business district. (Photo by author)

bankrupting as a result of drawn-out legal battles, and forced exile to hobble key opposition figures and undermine their political movements. Furthermore, the PAP faced the challenge of governing a multiethnic population that had been treated differentially by the British colonial administration and that maintained loyalties to other nations given that they were largely composed of recent migrants. To solidify their grip on power, build a new nation, and create what they considered to be the right conditions for multinational capital post-1965, the PAP continued to hammer away at its political opponents while demobilizing civil society at large, in ways tied especially to infrastructure creation. It developed, in these early years of Singapore's postcolonial era, a mode of governance characterized by the repression, manipulation, and co-optation of the population to clear the way for technocratic economic and urban development planning.

As already mentioned, the PAP engaged in campaigns to ruin key political opponents through various means so that it could shape the field of formal party politics in its favor. The party also placed serious limits on civil liberties for the population at large by legislating strict regulations on public speech, public assembly, and public behavior while bringing the media and the trade unions under state control. But sidelining overt detraction in these ways was only one part of its early policy efforts. Social and spatial engineering to ensure a stable pool of workers and PAP supporters was the centerpiece of the party's long game. As a city-state, Singapore's national development is tied to its urban development to an unusual extent, and the nation-state's government has an exceptional degree of control over the uses and reuses of urban space. Officially justified by problematic state discourses declaring the needs for "slum clearance" and a "takeoff" for modernization, Land Acquisition Acts were passed in 1966 and 1967. They made the public acquisition of land for the purposes of resettlement or industrialization (and at prices set by the government) compulsory, and they paved the way for the Singapore state to become the owner of the overwhelming majority of the city-state's land holdings by the mid-1970s. Early in the postcolonial period, therefore, the PAP could extensively redevelop the urban landscape, wiping out the segregated, sprawling housing stock that ringed the administrative center of the colonial city to actualize a new, "rational" master plan that rezoned commercial, industrial, and residential activities. Furthermore, while it built transport nodes, state-of-the-art industrial facilities, and scores of modern public housing apartment blocks, the PAP also unrolled new education, health, family planning, labor, and migration policies and programs all aimed at producing a nation of "modern" Singaporeans.

In terms of labor policies, the state took control of trade unions, lowered minimum wages, extended the work week, reduced annual and medical leave, and severely undermined the possibility of strikes (Liow 2011). Simultaneous innovations in other policy arenas wiped out informal economies and settlements and pushed Singapore citizens into formal employment. Flows of temporary migrants were completely suspended as the state worked at turning the former entrepôt comprising predominantly migrant workers into a nation of sedentary citizens, and these citizens were spatially reorganized via new public housing initiatives and policies. As Loh Kah Seng states, "Public housing, the quintessential architectural form of mid twentieth-century modernism, became the chief instrument of social change. . . . The aim was not, as frequently avowed, merely to raise the people's living standards, but to mould the semi-autonomous residents into model citizens of the high modernist nation-state" (2009, 140). By the end of the colonial era, most of the colonized population lived in unplanned and informal settlements in both the urban core and semiurban periphery. Cast by the colonial administration and then the PAP as "diseased" and "chaotic" areas of blight, and as obstacles to economic and social development efforts (see Loh 2009), these areas had in fact grounded the everyday social and political lives of Singapore's populace. Extended family and kinship networks thrived in these locales, as did clan and ethnic associations and a wide range of left-wing organizations. Resistance to resettlement was widespread but summarily quashed, while, as Gregory Clancey notes, the PAP represented resistant squatters as "dupes of 'agitators,' 'people out for mischief,' 'pro-Communist elements,' or in one colorful phrase, 'evil-wishers'" (2003, 19). Clancey further argues that housing reform in early postcolonial Singapore was fueled not just by concern for the poor, as the state then and still today insists, but also by fear of them. Through evictions and demolitions, the PAP broke up "an existing communalism seen to be identical with slums, *kampungs*, and squatter camps" (Clancey 2003, 20) and "atomized" subcommunities, especially racial and ethnic ones, while creating a class of home owners with a stake in the new nation and a vested interest in the continued growth of its economy. At the same time, the Central Provident Fund, a compulsory individual savings scheme, was established to impart a sense of responsibility and to further entrench a sense of the need and utility of buying in to the new system among the Singaporean populace, and to allow the state to avoid burdening itself with the provision of a strong social safety net. The PAP government, after all, has throughout its rule viewed welfarism as something that "would result in a general 'leveling' down of the population" (Chua 2010, 343).[3]

Also in relation to reconfiguring the everyday, private, home lives of the populace, the PAP set about to "upgrade" the family (Salaff 1988). While the British colonial legal system aimed to preserve the "traditional" marriage and family customs of Singapore's various ethnic communities, the PAP government set immediately to the task of "modernizing" these laws and policies to "bring order and uniformity into the prevailing legal chaos" (Kuo and Wong 1979, 8). The state became particularly obsessed with family planning. While population control was previously left to civil society organizations, the management of fertility received strong governmental support with the establishment of the Singapore Family Planning and Population Bureau in 1969. Among its efforts, voluntary sterilization and abortion were legalized and strong financial disincentives for large families were put in place (Drakakis-Smith et al. 1993). In addition, efforts to create a nation of "strong" families were given a significant boost by the newly established Housing Development Board (HDB). As the HDB began to roll out an extensive public housing program, eligibility for occupancy of flats was limited to those who formed a "proper family nucleus," with priority given to small families.[4] These aggressive antinatalist measures, however, worked all too well, driving the fertility level to below replacement level, and were followed by pronatalist initiatives since the late 1980s. Among these measures are the formation of the Social Development Unit (SDU, a national matchmaking agency), constant exhortations to marry and (then) procreate via the state-linked media, numerous programs of the Ministry of Community Youth and Sport to encourage the formation and maintenance of families, annual "Romancing Singapore" campaigns, the maintenance of "proper family nucleus" eligibility requirements for HDB flats (in which approximately 85 percent of the present citizenry resides), and more (Teo 2011).

Finally, the postcolonial PAP crafted its own version of multiracialism and multiculturalism to foster "social harmony" within its meritocratic system.

Singapore-style multiracialism is based on the arithmetic formula of four "separate" but "equal" races in a nation of "one people." As most of the population at the time of independence was a settler population (with Chinese, Malays, and Indians representing approximately 77 percent, 14 percent, and 8 percent of the new citizens, respectively), the PAP avoided any independence discourse asserting a return to indigenous roots (see Benjamin 1976). As Chua notes, "What was particular to Singapore was the fact that the largest ethnic group had no proprietary claim to the land, and the further fact that the nominally indigenous group was a distinct demographic minority. This demographic distribution meant that no conventional unity of race, land and culture could be evoked as the 'organic' basis for a new 'nation'" (2010, 337). Singapore's multiracial philosophy, which then as now was put in place largely through language and education policies and enforced through sedition laws,[5] thus propounds the need to submerge ethnic identity to the larger purposes of nation building and national identity construction while apparently providing space for each of the four founding ethnic groups to promote, valorize, and reclaim ethnic links and identity. Referred to as the Chinese-Malay-Indian-Others model, this form of multiculturalism continues colonial classificatory schemas drawn upon under British rule and underlies ethnic policies governing inter- and intra-ethnic relations in different spheres of life. It extends to government formulations of the Singapore nation to this day. For instance, in his vision of "building a multiracial nation through integration," then prime minister Goh Chok Tong states that the way forward for Singapore "is not mosaic pieces, but four overlapping circles. Each circle represents one community. The area where the circles overlap is the common area where we live, play and work together and where we feel truly Singaporean with minimal consciousness of our ethnicity. This pragmatic arrangement of seeking integration through overlapping circles has underwritten the racial and religious harmony that Singapore enjoys today" (2000, 16). Alternatively, Philip Holden, in line with other critical scholars, describes Singapore's multiracialism as "the designation of race as the primordial marker of cultural identity, the cultivation of racial consciousness through educational and social policies, and then the bringing together of different 'races' under a framework of state-sponsored multiracialism that accords the nation-state legitimacy of operating through a rationality that is 'above race'" (2008, 351; see also Goh et al. 2009).

　　Through these means, the PAP profoundly reworked the terms of urban citizenship to facilitate the growth of an industrial economy. It created a new, postcolonial Singapore landscape characterized by a strong state and a severely curtailed public sphere. As Clancey observes, "by the time The Left 'took to the streets' of Singapore in a last bid for power in the mid and late 1960s, 'the street' was in the process of disappearing." More broadly, Joshua Comaroff notes the PAP created a landscape "in which fringe subjects and nonconformist spaces were increasingly unwelcome" (2007, 63). While income and quality of living levels quickly rose in the early post-independence years, the masses were demobilized as the PAP put in place an "ideological state apparatus (ISA) to socialize and condition the people into thinking and behaving in ways conducive for the advancement of the interest of those at the helm of the developmental state" (Liow 2011, 246).

Refining the Global-Local Dynamic

The interventionist Singapore state is a self-described "pragmatic" one. It recognizes the changing nature of capitalist economies and the resultant need to constantly adapt to market realities to maintain continued economic growth. Thus, when growth flagged in Singapore in the late 1970s amid a global economic recession, the PAP reworked its economic plan. Throughout the 1980s, it moved to increase its "capture of value added in the process of production" by shifting from its "initial focus on labour-intensive manufacturing to more automated manufacturing" (Shatkin 2014, 119). This second phase of postcolonial Singapore's economic development was also importantly one of regionalization (see Low 2001; Olds and Yeung 2004). By the early 1980s, the pain and political complications from the failed Malaysia merger were to some extent alleviated, and Singapore's astounding economic growth and rise in stature on the global stage made it a desirable partner for its immediate neighbors. Particularly, economic ties with Malaysia and Indonesia were strengthened, bringing benefits to Singapore such as access to natural resources and the ability to move aspects of the production process offshore at a time when sustained economic growth since the mid-1960s had increased production costs at home (in 1989, these relationships were solidified and deepened with the formation of the Indonesia-Malaysia-Singapore growth triangle; on this, see Sparke et al. 2004). These two states, as well as China, were the major partners in Singapore's regionalization drive alongside other minor players (Leifer 2000). Importantly, this second economic development phase of Singapore's postcolonial era involved significant demographic changes. Whereas the previous export-oriented industrialization phase of economic development hinged on the sedentarization of the population to create a local working class, the regionalization phase saw the rise of a new class that was both upwardly and outwardly mobile. As the industrial economy matured, Singaporeans were pulled into the managerial ranks in factories and government-linked companies both locally and abroad. A sizeable group of Singaporeans thus lived and worked overseas for the first time in the city-state's postcolonial era, and migrant workers began to flow into Singapore to do the jobs that Singaporeans, given the new existence among them of an enlarged middle class, had begun to leave behind.

This reconfiguration of the city-state's economy to rely on global flows of capital, goods, *and* people posed challenges to the PAP's carefully calibrated post-1965 social order. As outlined above, the PAP pulled a vast array of policy levers to build a *cohesive* Singaporean identity, polity, and economy out of a disparate group of (mostly) settlers. The reworking of the nation's relationship to global forces in its second post-independence economic phase threw up certain challenges to the state's dominant unifying discourse. Emerging class differences and the migration of large numbers of "foreigners" into the city-state (even if admitted almost primarily on temporary work visas at that point) and of Singaporeans out of Singapore began to forge new dividing lines, which would grow over time such that the PAP has dealt with them in earnest throughout Singapore's third phase of economic development. I will turn to that phase shortly. First, though, it must be noted that during the 1980s, top-down notions of nationhood and national belonging began to shift in important ways.

As Michael Barr and Jevon Low note, Singapore's version of multiracialism through the 1970s was "based on a presumption that Singapore's future lay with assimilating her [*sic*] various ethnic cultures into a dominant hegemonic culture" (2005, 162). But "around the end of the 1970s, the beginnings of a shift from a communally neutral assimilation to a society dominated by overt manifestations of 'Chineseness' could be seen in public statements and public actions emanating from the government" (Barr and Low 2005, 165). State discourse, stemming especially from then prime minister Lee Kuan Yew, on the merits of emanating the purported traits of Singapore's Chinese community began to emerge. One way in which this preference for the Chinese community came through in dramatic fashion was the Graduate Mothers' Scheme of 1984. As noted above, family planning became a core part of Singapore's social engineering efforts in 1966, but initial antinatalist efforts were so successful that by the early 1980s, fertility rates had dropped below replacement level. The PAP, as part of its shift to pronatalist policies, then introduced a program that sought to encourage women with university degrees to bear children (through, for example, tax incentives, preferences for school placement for the children born of graduate mothers). Upon accusations that the program showed preference for the Chinese majority, given its higher educational attainment levels in comparison with Malay and Indian communities and derision of the large families of minority groups, this specific program was scrapped (Heng and Devan 1995). But, as discussed in chapter 4, the aims of the scheme lived on in other family planning policies and programs. Also, Lee launched the "Speak Mandarin" campaign in 1979. The Singapore government has maintained a policy of bilingual education since 1966, under which Singaporeans learn both English and their designated "mother tongue"—Mandarin, Malay, and Tamil for Chinese, Malay, and Indian Singaporeans respectively. But Lee was displeased with persistently low national levels of competency in Mandarin as a second language by the late 1970s, in part due to the use of Chinese dialects in home spaces, and thus rolled out the extensive and still ongoing Speak Mandarin campaign. The official rationale for the program is that Mandarin is economically valuable given China's rise as a major force in the global economy, and that learning Mandarin helps bring Chinese Singaporeans together by forging some sort of transhistorical, essential tie across dialect groups.

As the PAP undertook its "modernization" program in the 1960s, it may have looked globally for foreign capital sources, but it relied on a discourse of generic "Asian values" to set its modernization project apart from the rest and to keep its population grounded as flows of foreign capital, goods, and cultural influences entered this nascent global city. As Comaroff notes, the new, postcolonial landscape was "recognizably a Singaporean invention, but without falling prey to pedigree, a specificity without specifics" (2007, 62; see also Wee 2007). The prioritization of Chineseness and Chinese language is thus striking in this new nation overtly built on the stated principles of meritocracy and race neutrality, especially given that the government's insistence that its political sphere operates "above race" has been formalized in all kinds of ways. For instance, the public housing resettlement schemes already discussed aimed explicitly to break up racial and ethnic enclaves to undermine racial and ethnic factionalism in everyday life. Also in the mid- to late 1960s, political organizing along racial lines was effectively prohibited through the enactment of various policies and laws (see Goh and Holden 2009). The PAP affirmed that civil society organizations across the board must not engage in politics, and this includes organizations formed along racial and/or ethnic lines. Racial and ethnic groups can organize only as benevolent associations formed under and/or at the behest of the government (see Barr 2003).[6] Furthermore, toward the end of the regionalization phase of Singapore's economic development, in the late 1980s, the PAP enacted two new policies that significantly furthered the officially "race neutral" nature of Singapore politics. In 1989 it established ethnic quotas for individual HDB housing blocks (see Sin 2003), and in 1992 it changed its electoral system such that citizens vote not for individuals for Parliament, but for a team of candidates called a Group Representation Constituency (GRC). The composition of each GRC is balanced to include people of all of Singapore's major ethnic/racial groups in the same proportions as each group composes the national population.

The stated aim of these policies is to maintain "racial harmony" and to "stunt any tendency towards the inflammation of racial tensions" (Barr 2003, 80). These are important and laudable goals. But, as many critics point out, the Singapore state strives to achieve "racial harmony" in a top-down manner, and its multicultural and multiracial policies are deployed as part of a wide-ranging ideological state apparatus. As Chua notes, "The 'risk' of disrupting harmony has rendered the entire domain of 'race' a politically 'sensitive' domain," and "racial harmony thus operates as a repressive device for pre-empting public debate and sustained negotiation of the issues that commonly plague a multiracial society" (2010, 346–347). It also, as Barr notes, places limits on interethnic and interracial discourse since Singapore's notion of multiculturalism asserts that racial and ethnic groups are discreet and essential and "stops other elements of civil society, such as trade unions, from addressing questions of ethnic injustice" (2003, 80).

Furthermore, as an effort to bolster the official ideology of multiculturalism and stem the growth of the fractures that began to build throughout the region-alization phase of postcolonial Singapore's economic development trajectory, the PAP produced a white paper on "Shared Values" in 1991. The state adopted the four values included in the original document and thereafter added a fifth, national ideology. The five values are (1) nation before community and society above self; (2) family as the basic unit of society; (3) community support and respect for the individual; (4) consensus, not conflict; and (5) racial and religious harmony. The document, though, broadly emphasized the general will of the community and consensual politics over liberal rights and individual interests, and the Shared Values were explicitly advanced to curb "Western" influences and maintain "Asian values." Consistent with the PAP's modus operandi of in-tensively intervening simultaneously in economic and social life, the adoption of the Shared Values accompanied the publication of Singapore's 1991 Strategic Economic Plan by the Ministry of Trade and Industry. This plan "established the target to 'catch up' with the per capita Gross National Product of a 'first league developed country' in the years 2020–2030" (Goh and Holden 2009, 8) and was put forward in tandem with the white paper with the stated aim of making Singapore "a developed country in every sense" (Singapore Ministry of Trade and Industry, quoted in Goh and Holden 2009, 9).[7] The clear intention here was to bolster the climate of "race neutrality," "social harmony," and "depolit-icization" that was created in the late 1960s and early 1970s and to undermine the articulation of alternative visions of Singapore's developmental path as eco-nomic growth proceeded apace and the PAP worried that the legitimacy of and tolerance for a strong state would wane as a middle and managerial class grew (Goh and Holden 2009). These concerns have remained in place throughout the third economic phase in Singapore's postcolonial era, which I turn to now.

A Creative Turn

Singapore's global economic competitiveness waned in the 1990s, particularly in the wake of the 1997 Asian Financial Crisis. The always-interventionist PAP then devised new plans and began to enact the transition to the "globalized, entrepreneurial, diversified" economy that it still today asserts will bring Sin-gapore successfully into the future (Singapore Ministry of Trade and Industry 2003). The core of this new economic phase has been the careful nurturing and prioritization of a knowledge-based economy. For instance, efforts to become a global education hub have been extensive, entailing the opening of new universities, the expansion of existing universities, and the formalization of institutional linkages with various foreign universities (see Lim 2009; Olds 2007). The cultivation of a reputation as a "global city for the arts" is well under way, with the opening of the Esplanade—Theatres by the Bay, an arts complex in downtown Singapore containing a concert hall, several smaller theaters, outdoor stages, and many restaurants, as well as the creation and promotion of numerous arts festivals and funding for arts education (see Chang 2000; Tan 2007b). The city-state is now also an important biotechnology hub, in large part due to the creation of Biopolis, a life sciences center launched to put key Singaporean biomedical research institutes into contact with biotechnology and pharmaceutical companies on the local and global stages (see Waldby 2009).

This new economy of course requires a new sort of worker and the pulling of workers from many places. So the Singapore government, in the role it assumes as manager of human resources for multinational capital, joined the global competition for "talent" in earnest. In his 1999 National Day speech, then-PM Goh expressed this aim clearly: "We must make Singapore an oasis of talent. Many cities are vying to be the key global node in the region—Hong Kong, Shanghai, Sydney, Taipei, Singapore. Who wins depends on who attracts the most talent" (Goh 1999).[8] Recall that the government effectively closed its borders to foreign migrants in the early independence years. As industrialization gathered steam in the 1970s, immigration controls were relaxed and inflows of "unskilled" laborers—or what the Singapore government refers to as "foreign workers"— from countries such as the Philippines, Indonesia, Thailand, India, Bangladesh, and Sri Lanka were allowed for. The numbers of such immigrants were small throughout this decade. In the knowledge-based economy era, though, flows of "foreign workers" have become increasingly central to Singapore's development efforts as it needs to fill positions in the low-level service sector and in the construction and domestic work arenas. In addition, the transition from a manufacturing-based to a service sector economy in the 1980s initiated an inflow of great numbers of "skilled" foreign laborers—known in Singapore as "foreign talent." Overall, from 2.9 percent of the population in 1970 (Yeoh 2006), the total share of the nonresident population rose to approximately 5 percent in 1980, 10 percent in 1990, and 19 percent in 2000. In absolute terms, the nonresident population was 131,820 in 1980, 331,264 in 1990, and 754,524 in 2000 (see Teo and Piper 2009).

To attract and retain "talent" (both foreign and local), as PM Lee Hsien Loong stated in 2005, the Singapore government also embraced the "need to remake our city, so that it is vibrant, cosmopolitan and throbbing with energy, with our own distinctive X-factor that makes us stand out from other cities" (Lee 2005). Phenomenal changes to the urban landscape have been effected since the 1990s. These include the infrastructural investments in universities, arts centers, and so on mentioned above, as well as much more. "Lifestyle quarters" such as One-North and South Beach are in various stages of development (figure 1.2). Leisure areas such as the Singapore River, Dempsey Road, and Sentosa have been revitalized. Green spaces and parks have been developed throughout the island. The city's marina area got a remarkable facelift and now hosts the soaring Marina Bay Sands Hotel and Casino (figure 1.3), numerous leisure sites, and a new downtown financial district on reclaimed land. Finally, enclave urbanism in the form of private housing developments and "upgrading" of public housing complexes to offer housing options for upwardly mobile Singaporeans is extensive.[9]

This emphasis on "talent" and the clear linkage to urban redevelopment strategies exemplifies the Singapore government's serious engagement with the ideas popularized by economic geographer and urban policy advisor Richard Florida, among others, on the notion of creative cities. As is by now widely known, Florida (2002) argues that a "creative class"—his term for "talent"—powers urban and regional economic growth. Thus, he suggests that business incentives and downtown revitalization projects aimed at luring capital to specific urban locales are insufficient without also taking measures to attract those who might work for local firms or start up their own "new economy" enterprises. In brief, he argues in *The Rise of the Creative Class* that a city must have "buzz" to surge to the forefront in today's knowledge-based global economy. Various urban studies scholars have questioned Florida's argument on numerous grounds—including methodological and empirical critiques, political/social equity concerns, and questions about the reproducibility of "creative city" strategies (Krätke 2011; Luckman, Gibson, and Lea 2009; Markusen 2006; Peck 2005)—and Florida himself moved away from prescribing the fostering of the "creative class" as a panacea for urban problems in his recent work (see Florida 2017). Nonetheless, Singapore's government has taken up the notion of creative urbanism enthusiastically, and, as noted above, the city-state's resulting facelift has been astounding.

In taking on board Florida's notion that creative economies are fueled by the presence in large numbers of members of the "creative class" and that such persons are attracted to places with urban buzz, the PAP has also taken seriously the notion that urban buzz is fostered best where there is a certain degree of societal openness. In Florida's argument, the creative class prefers to settle in places that have innovative, diverse, and tolerant cultures: "Creative people are attracted to, and high-tech industry takes root in, places that score high on our basic indicators of diversity—the Gay, Bohemian and other indexes. . . . Why would this be so? It is not because high-tech industries are populated by great numbers of bohemians and gay people. Rather, artists, musicians, gay people and the members of the Creative Class in general prefer places that are open and diverse" (2002, 250).[10] Florida advises that to create the right nonmarket/quality of life conditions, therefore, cities must nurture what he refers to as the "3Ts" of economic development—technology, talent, and tolerance. The PAP

FIGURE 1.2. South Beach, Singapore's new lifestyle quarter. (Photo by author)

FIGURE 1.3. Rendering of the Marina Bay Sands Integrated Resort from the 2008 Singapore Draft Master Plan Exhibit at the Urban Redevelopment Authority. (Photo by author)

has thus recognized a need to manage Singapore culture and society differently and has engaged in what Kenneth Paul Tan describes as the "sexing up" of Singapore to fit this bill. As Tan notes, it has been persuaded that the new economy requires that "cosmopolitan Singaporeans, foreign investors, global talent and tourists must . . . feel that Singapore is a sexy, funky and cool place in which to live, work, play and visit" (Tan 2003, 418). He further observes, "The government needs to anchor Singaporeans who possess skills that are in global demand and an outlook that enables them to settle almost anywhere in the world, since these 'cosmopolitans'—together with similarly talented foreigners working in the country—are needed to fuel Singapore's new economy, of which the creative industries will make up a large part" (Tan 2007a, 26).

To foster the buzz that purportedly serves as the anchor for this creative class, Singapore's government has adapted its political strategies along with its economic ones. It has done this, as Goh Chok Tong states, to encourage "greater risk-taking, experimentation, diversity, choices and decision" among its populace (quoted in Yao 2007, 24). It now aims to foster an "active" citizenry, as PM Lee Hsien Loong stated in 2004: "We will encourage Singaporeans to participate more actively in solving their own problems, and to organize themselves to do their part for their community. An active citizenry will help us to build a national consensus, engender a sense of rootedness, and enable the Government to serve the people better" (quoted in Tan 2007a, 28). This effort to open up Singapore's public culture has been manifold, ranging from high-profile and extensive public consultation exercises such as "Remaking Singapore" to the lifting of bans on bar-top dancing, bungee jumping, and gambling.[11] Yet, the PAP still very much constrains the advancement of political alternatives while insisting on the maintenance of core traditional values. As Tan and Jin state, "Basically, the government only wants enough liberalization to keep the foreign and local creative class satisfied so that the economy will grow, but not the kind of liberalization that amounts to political pluralism—the political opposition in Singapore continues to fight uphill battles just to win a handful of seats in parliament" (2007, 199). So, although Singapore now has "buzz" and its creative economy is thriving, significant political changes have not followed.

As this brief overview of postcolonial Singapore through its three main economic phases to date shows, its development has been much more than an economic feat. It is also a product of deliberate political strategies and extensive social engineering initiatives. Or, as Shatkin eloquently states, "The adoption of the Singapore model has generally been based on the fallacy that it is fundamentally a model of urban design, architecture, and infrastructure development, which can be achieved simply by gaining control of a piece of land and redeveloping it in the Singapore mold. In fact, I will argue, it has been the capacity of the Singaporean state to revolutionize the terms of urban citizenship through its dominance of land and economy that marks the Singapore model as distinct" (2014, 118). In the early postcolonial decades, the PAP developed its own unique governance style. Commentators disagree on whether to label it authoritarianism, "soft authoritarianism" (Nasir and Turner 2013), or something else, such as Chua Beng Huat's "anti-liberal democracy with a communitarian ethos" (Chua 1995). Regardless, consensus is that the developmental Singapore state has loomed large over Singapore society throughout its postcolonial period. As Chua notes, "Singapore's successful capitalist economic development . . . is by now legend. Lesser known are the cultural underpinnings of that growth. A set of prerequisite cultural values and appropriate attitudes had to be inculcated in the population of Singapore in order for the economy to take off and for subsequent sustained growth. . . . A massive cultural transformation was necessary to bring the population in line with the cultural requirements of capitalist industrialization" (Chua 1995, 1). Otherwise put, Singapore governance can be understood as "above all a cultural practice . . . managed through a range of discourses and semiotic practices which create the requisite ideological positions" (Goh 2005, 20; see also Wee 2007).

The PAP treats culture as a residual factor that can be instrumentally manipulated for the achievement of desired economic ends, and "the ability of the government to exercise such tight control of society, and the basis on which the population accepts this direction, have been central to Singapore's economic success" (Perry, Kong, and Yeoh 1997: 7). The workforce that the PAP offered up as an attraction for multinational capital in its early postcolonial decades was a well-disciplined one, and the government approached cultural concerns—such as multiculturalism and gender differences—as bureaucratic matters to be dealt with from the top down (see Ang and Stratton 1995; Lyons 2004b). As Lee Kuan Yew stated in 1987, "I am often accused of interfering in the private lives of citizens. Yes, if I did not, had I not done that, we wouldn't be here today. And I say without the slightest remorse, that we wouldn't be here, we would not have made economic progress, if we had not intervened on very personal matters—who your neighbour is, how you live, the noise you make, how you spit, or what language you use. We decide what is right."[12] With the emphasis thus firmly placed on fostering structural efficiencies even in its current knowledge-based economy era, the Singapore success story remains in large part a story of the emergence and maintenance of a strong and heavily interventionist state.

The contemporary PAP compels Singaporean citizens to constantly adapt and change in pursuit of continued economic growth, while far-reaching social control measures curb and contain civil liberties and curtail access to public goods in all kinds of ways. Overarching ideologies of racial harmony, shared values, and meritocracy persist in the city-state, as do laws limiting free speech, public assembly, and political organizing, while state ideology is promoted through a wide array of state programs. As Pow Choon-Piew accurately notes, "Virtually every sphere of Singapore society bears the indelible imprint of state policies" (2013, 185). In its "new economy"/"active citizenship"/"urban buzz" era, the Singapore state thus remains strong. It still exerts considerable efforts to fold civil society under its large umbrella, and it still exercises extraordinary control over urban space while creating spaces for new economic activities. Yet much has changed in terms of its standing with Singaporeans since the PAP's early days in power when it was widely and deeply unpopular due to the ruthless ways in which it toppled political opponents to get into office. Over time, the PAP has come to be perceived as a relevant and efficient purveyor of economic growth and well-being. While its extensive social engineering efforts have politically "immobilized the masses" (see Trocki 2006), Singaporeans have long enjoyed a very high average standard of living under the PAP and most are now part of a consumer class. Even though Singapore is not a welfare state, the PAP has always used surplus growth to provide social goods such as housing, health care, and education and thus to achieve political legitimacy. Opposition parties have multiplied and even gained some ground in recent elections, but the promise of persistent economic growth and social stability under the PAP (as well as the withholding of government resources from districts that elect opposition party representatives) has kept the party firmly in government. The PAP has, in other words, proven its staying power. While many questioned how long this heavily interventionist developmental state could last, especially as it entered the knowledge-based economy phase, it is going strong as a "neoliberal-developmental state" (Liow 2011).

This narrative of Singapore's postcolonial economic development and social engineering efforts may, to the reader unfamiliar with the city-state, seem rather closed. That is because, as urban scholar Jane M. Jacobs noted in 2015,

> there is something about the speed and efficiency, thoroughness and, actually, often the sheer quality of the execution and realization of Singaporean visions that can literally suck the air out of things—take up all the space, literally and metaphori-cally—and leave no oxygen or room for alternative dreams, or for futures thinking that is not packaged as a national vision, a set of shared values, a series of agreed upon benchmark targets, or earnestly reached for performance indicators.[13]

Yet, desires for other paths persist in Singapore, as do efforts to create spaces in which these desires can be expressed; and, while the government remains resistant to change, the slight liberalization of the polity and the fostering of "creative" sectors like arts and education at least mean that civil society and public discourse are more robust than ever before in Singapore's postcolonial history. Indeed, Jacobs made her critical remarks at a conference put on by Singapore's Asian Urban Lab, a registered nonprofit organization founded in 2003.[14] Titled "Singapore Dreaming," it was a "ground up initiative" that brought together academics, artists, and other professionals to "explore alternative visions of a Singapore that is sustainable, creative and vibrant," to provide an opportunity to "think the unthinkable, and to formulate new possibilities."[15] In addition, local community-based and nongovernmental organizations concerned with gender issues, migrant worker issues, poverty and economic inequality, discrimination against LGBT persons, and more have flourished in recent years. Alternate media outlets, largely internet based, have also emerged to expand the scope of public discourse. While examination of all these civil society mobilizations is beyond the scope of this chapter, I turn now to close it with a nod to the growth of a critical Singapore studies literature in recent decades, as a segue into the queer critique of this global city that is developed in the chapters that follow.

Whose Global City Is It?

My narration in this chapter of the general contours of Singapore's global city project since 1965 relies heavily on existing critical Singapore studies scholarship. There is of course much, much more work than that which I have cited here. The field has grown tremendously in recent decades as Singapore has gained prominence globally and loosened restrictions on academic freedom for the sake of its knowledge economy (on the latter, see Olds 2012). An overriding theme in this literature is critique of the city-state government's relentless pursuit of economic growth while it curtails personal freedoms. Commentators interested in a wide range of topics and coming from various disciplines especially question whether social and political changes in Singapore's current creative city era offer possibilities for progressive social change. Since the PAP long ago set up a calculus whereby its legitimacy stems from its ability to deliver sustained economic growth, and it continues to strongly intervene in the personal lives of its citizens to attain this goal, many question whether the system can persist now that it is not simply a "developmental state" but a "neoliberal-developmental state" (Liow 2011) with a decentralized economy promoting an "entrepreneurial culture." Or, as Shatkin puts it, many consider whether the PAP can "engage citizens in governance and define a distinct and vibrant Singaporean culture without compromising the overriding goal of PAP political control" (2014, 123).

There is a wealth of scholarly work that explores how the dramatic transformations of Singapore's social and economic landscape are negotiated by its citizens. Predominant questions that run through the literature are who the new neoliberal-developmental Singapore citizen is, and whether social tensions coming to the fore in the contemporary city-state have the potential to be democratizing ones. Recent work focuses on the ways that various subjects caught up in the latest phase of Singapore's global city project negotiate their roles within it. Students (Cheng 2015), "foreign talent" (Montsion 2012), "foreign migrants" (Kitiarsa 2008; Yea 2017), Singaporeans in diaspora (Ho 2006, 2011), gated community residents (Pow 2011, 2013), environmental activists (Neo 2007), artists (Luger 2016), women (Yeoh and Willis 2005), the poor (Teo 2016), LGBT people (Tan 2016), and everyday urban dwellers (Chang and Huang 2011; Muzaini and Yeoh 2007) are some of those whose lives in global city Singapore shape scholarly views on the city-state now. Overall, this literature reports instances of both complicities and contestations, of investments in the status quo and resistances against it. The jury, in short, is still out on whether and how sweeping progressive social changes might be enacted in the city-state.

There is thus still very much a need for critical analyses of the forces perpetuating social injustices in Singapore. To this end, the literature cited in this chapter (and much more) offers potent critiques of elitism, racism and ethnocentrism, nationalism, patriarchy, and heterosexism. But it does not offer a critique of heteronormativity as distinct from heterosexism, as a confluence of sexual norms with race, class, gender norms, and more. On this point, I turn in the next chapter to the "gay debates" that have raged in Singapore since the early 2000s, to start building the case for the need for a queer critique of this global city.

CHAPTER 2

Singapore as "Straight Space"

"Someday," begins the 2012 campaign video for Pink Dot, the event that has brought together LGBT Singaporeans and their supporters for an annual public assembly in the city-state's Hong Lim Park since 2009.[1] "Someday, it won't matter to the world if I'm gay or straight," says a teacher who dreams of another place in time when his colleagues and students accept his same-sex relationship. He is snapped back from this reverie as a photo on his desk of the teacher and his partner, smiling and holding their dog, is replaced by a photo that closes in on the dog alone. Next, a trans woman overhears unkind chatter as she leaves a public restroom. She states, "Someday, nobody will stare or point fingers or call names." Then we move to a family gathering, where a young woman enjoys a meal with her parents and female partner. That fantasy is broken by a cut to a scene of the same parents instead wrapped in an anguished embrace while they sit across from their daughter, with a pamphlet titled "understanding homosexuality" resting on the table between them. The daughter states, "Someday, our partners will be a part of our families." The video goes on to invoke a "someday" when "gay people will be free to express themselves without censorship," a "someday" when "a new chapter will be written for the gay people of Singapore." But "while we wait for someday to arrive," says the voice-over, "we can do our part today to make society more inclusive and open-minded. We can take a stand against discrimination and prejudice. We can join hands to support the right of every Singaporean to love. Every year with Pink Dot, we celebrate a solidarity in diversity. Every day with Pink Dot, we bring that someday a little closer. And as more and more of us stand up to be counted, the sooner that someday will come. So see you at Pink Dot 2012. Let us make someday happen." This video unfortunately speaks to an all too common situation in the global scheme of things. While LGBT rights gains in certain contexts over the last few decades have been remarkable, sexual minorities still endure legal and policy inequities in most of the world's countries, including Singapore. Activist efforts to instigate legislative and policy changes that would institutionalize LGBT nondiscrimination have been definitively dismissed by the PAP government. As such, Pink Dot makes a necessary plea for equity and open-mindedness with its call for the "freedom to love."

From another angle, however, Pink Dot's vision of the future, and indeed this activist organization's very existence, is quite extraordinary. As recently as the late 1990s, Singapore's government went to great lengths to stamp out same-sex sexual activities and discourage LGBT community building. The removal of liquor licenses of several bars frequented by gay and lesbian clientele were rumored to be ordered by the government; police raids of gay bars and cruising grounds were well publicized and led to multiple arrests, caning sentences, and the publication of entrapped men's pictures in local newspapers; and censorship restrictions pertaining to literature, film, television, and theater kept representations of LGBT persons largely out of the public sphere (Heng 2001). Furthermore, in 1997, members of the LGBT advocacy organization People Like Us were brought in for police questioning after their application for registration as an official society was flatly denied.[2] So the existence of Pink Dot as an activist initiative that has gone from drawing a crowd of twenty-five hundred in 2009 to twenty-eight thousand in 2016 and is able to make a public call for LGBT inclusion evidences a significant change.

This change began in the early 2000s. Shortly after the publication of his book *The Rise of the Creative Class* in 2002, urban economic policy advisor Richard Florida visited Singapore to give public talks and meet with policy makers in various government ministries. Around the same time, a spate of articles on his ideas about creative cities as tolerant cities appeared in the main daily newspaper the *Straits Times*, a media outlet that like all those in the city-state is run with strong government ties and oversight.[3] One representative article, titled "Making Room for the Three T's," states, "For Singapore to thrive economically, it must accept immigrant talent, artists, and homosexuals. . . . The creative class wants to be where there is a happening scene, a pulsating music and arts environment, and a tolerant and diverse population. . . . [A] city needs to focus on getting the right 'people climate'" (*Straits Times* 2002).[4] In subsequent months and years, as part of the fostering of a new knowledge-based, creative economy and accompanying efforts to create a cityscape that has "buzz," and despite the critiques of Florida's approach that I discussed in chapter 1, the city-state government embraced Richard Florida's mantra that tolerance attracts talent in part by liberalizing its stance on sexual difference to project a global image of gay-friendliness.[5]

As a result, although the disenfranchisement of sexual minorities persists in Singapore, local LGBT subcultures and community/activist organizations now flourish and the city-state has quite surprisingly come to be popularly known as Asia's "new gay capital" (Yue 2007). In other words, as PM Lee stated in a speech to Parliament in 2007 to announce his government's decision to reject activist calls for the repeal of Section 377A of the Singapore Penal Code (a colonial-era statute prohibiting "gross indecency" between two men), "the tone of the overall society . . . remains conventional, it remains straight" and, as such, "there is space, and there are limits." In this chapter, I examine this impasse. I interrogate why in this time of LGBT tolerance in Singapore's history it is still represented by the PAP as an officially "straight" space, and what specifically this designation means in the context of this contemporary city-state and leading "global city."

My ability to explore these questions stems from the fact that unprecedented recent public debates on homosexuality in the city-state have opened up space for critical reflection (and note that I use the term "homosexuality" here because, as demonstrated in what follows, the public debates that I highlight focus on the topic of the merits and demerits of homosexuality versus heterosexuality). Furthermore, my drive to explore them stems from a desire to build on the remarkable activist and community efforts that congeal in Singapore's local LGBT movement. The mere existence of Pink Dot and many other Singaporean LGBT organizations is heartening, and their joint efforts to improve the plight of sexual minorities deserve much praise. These groups offer necessary and vibrant critiques of homophobia, transphobia, and heterosexism, they play a pivotal role in putting issues of equity on the basis of sexual and gender identity into mainstream public debate, and they doubtless enrich the everyday lives of many LGBT Singaporeans in profound ways. Even though there is still a long way to go in terms of effecting legal and policy change, these are no small feats. In what follows, I build on the work of these organizations, and on the small body of existing queer studies work on the city-state (see, for instance, Lim 2005a; Lim 2004; Lo and Huang 2003; Tan 2009; Weiss 2005; Yue and Zubillaga-Pow 2012) to contribute to the advocacy efforts on behalf of LGBT people in Singapore and more. I say "and more" because while there is no doubt that homophobia and transphobia are real and rife and need combating (even in contexts in which equal rights have been won for LGBT persons), queer scholars and activists caution the need for scrutiny rather than straightforward celebration. For sexual politics is never only about the policing of a heterosexual-homosexual binary, and the march of progress thus entails the pitting of the properly domestic against the "queer" even when LGBT people make it in from the margins.[6]

In this chapter, I consider the debates over the place of homosexuality in Singapore, describing their unfolding, contextualizing them within the government's plans for a bright future of creative urbanism, and outlining the broad contours of critical activist and scholarly responses to date. It is worth noting here that throughout the chapter, I focus on setting out the PAP government's response to calls for LGBT equality. I do so not to suggest that the government and LGBT organizations are the only actors involved. There has also been anti-LGBT mobilization in Singapore society, particularly from evangelical groups. But while the Singapore government does take some heed of this countermovement's claims, as I point out later in this chapter, it states that its policy is guided more by socioeconomic concerns than by this faction's views. After discussing the sexual-identity-based project that has so far been the focus of local activism and critical commentary, I shift gears to think through what these debates over the place of LGBT persons in the city-state illuminate about the broader politics of intimacy that drives its global city project. In other words, in this chapter I think both with and against existing debates over the place of homosexuality in the city-state to move from their focus to date on sexual identity politics as a single issue to a broader set of concerns about the governance of family, home, kinship, love, and more.

Progress Narratives

Increasingly, critical commentators seeking social justice for sexual minorities in Singapore have asked where LGBT Singaporeans fit into the progress narrative. On this question, there have been direct answers from each of the three men who have held the city-state's office of prime minister. In 1998, Lee Kuan Yew, in his capacity as senior minister, was being interviewed live on CNN when he was asked the following question by an unnamed man in the call-in portion of the program: "I am a gay man in Singapore. I do not feel that my country has acknowledged my presence. As we move into a more tolerant millennium, what do you think is the future for gay people in Singapore, if there is a future at all?" Lee responded,

> Well, it's not a matter which I can decide or any government can decide. It's a question of what a society considers acceptable. And as you know, Singaporeans are by and large a very conservative, orthodox society, and very, I would say, completely different from, say, the United Sates and I don't think an aggressive gay rights movement would help. But what we are doing as a government is to leave people to live their own lives so long as they don't impinge on other people. I mean, we don't harass anybody. (quoted in Peterson 2001, 129–130)

He could have added "anymore" to his last sentence. As noted above, the PAP government went to considerable lengths to limit same-sex sexual activities and efforts to build LGBT community through much of the 1990s. But Lee was right; by 1998, these forms of government harassment had ceased. Furthermore, his response to the caller's question marked the first time that a senior government official had spoken about sexual minorities in a noncondemnatory tone.

Singapore's second prime minister, Goh Chok Tong, made a much bolder pronouncement some years later. In July 2003, a *Time Asia* magazine article written by author and journalist Simon Elegant and titled "The Lion in Winter" detailed the Singapore government's efforts to shake off the city-state's authoritarian image and foster an entrepreneurial, creative spirit in the face of changing global economic conditions and rising local unemployment rates. Toward the end of the article, Elegant writes,

> Repressive government policies previously enforced in the name of social stability are being relaxed. The city now boasts seven saunas catering almost exclusively to gay clients, for example, something unthinkable even a few years ago. There are a sprinkling of gay bars, and many dance clubs set aside one night each week for gay customers. Prime Minister Goh says his government now allows gay employees into its ranks, even in sensitive positions. The change in policy . . . is being implemented without fanfare, Goh says, to avoid raising the hackles of more-conservative Singaporeans. "So let it evolve, and in time the population will understand that some people are born that way," Goh says. "We are born this way and they are born that way, but they are like you and me." (Elegant 2003)

It must be noted that this "change in policy" was not a literal change in policy. Meredith Weiss quotes from her correspondence with a representative of the Public Service Division of the Prime Minister's Office who explains that the comment "was not a shift in policy . . . but an elaboration of the Singapore Civil Service's position on the employment policy of homosexuals," a position that they can be employed, as everyone else, based on "the principle of meritocracy" (Weiss 2005, 271n24). Regardless, this unprecedented and unexpected statement of tolerance was a watershed and spurred on a tremendous amount of local and international public debate.

Furthermore, unlike Lee Kuan Yew's 1998 statement, Goh's 2003 statement was not off the cuff, and its appearance in the "Lion in Winter" article made evident the rationale behind the government's deliberate move toward tolerance. The article deals in a general sense with the then new initiatives to transform the manufacturing base that spurred on Singapore's early economic growth into a postindustrial, knowledge-based economy. More specifically, it lays out the pivotal role that "talent" plays within this broad strategy. Indeed, the text that directly precedes the quote above is this: "Singapore will do 'whatever it takes' to attract talent, says Vivian Balakrishnan, the government official in charge of the Remaking Singapore Committee."[7] And the text that directly proceeds from it expands on this assertion as follows: "Authorities are trying to diversify the island's gene pool so that spontaneous change can occur. Once notoriously picky about whom it allowed into the country to live and work, Singapore has opened the floodgates in recent years through its 'foreign-talent' program. Foreigners, gay or straight, will be critical to carving out the niches in which the government hopes Singapore's new economy will thrive." The assertion that both "gay and straight" foreigners would be equally welcome has proven incorrect. Foreigners are allowed to migrate with opposite-sex dependent partners only (at least those in the "talent" category; see chapter 4 for discussion of the fact that those in the "worker" category are not allowed to bring any dependents). But the drive for "talent" in the context of Singapore's creative city push has indeed reshaped the city-state's economic and urban landscapes in multiple and profound ways, not least spurring on a move toward an official stance of tolerance toward sexual minorities.

This official statement of newfound tolerance led to much public debate. In fact, as Chris Tan notes, the public debate "became so heated that Goh had to order the local media to stop reporting on it a month later during his annual National Day Rally speech" (Tan 2009, 134). During that August 2003 speech, Goh qualified his earlier comments:

> As for my comments on gays, they do not signal any change in policy. That would erode the moral standards of Singapore, or our family values. In every society, there are gay people. We should accept those in our midst as fellow human beings, and as fellow Singaporeans. . . . That said, let me stress that I do not encourage or endorse a gay lifestyle. Singapore is still a traditional and conservative Asian society. Gays must know that the more they lobby for public space, the bigger the backlash they will provoke from the conservative mainstream. Their public space may then be reduced. (Goh 2003)

Thus the public sphere for gays and lesbians was pried slightly open, while LGBT activists and individuals were clearly told to stay in line.

In the mid-2000s, LGBT organizations and community groups, many of them nascent, tested the limits of the new tolerance. In the wake of Goh's statement, several small events and functions were held without censure; most notably, In-digNation—also known as "Singapore's Pride season"—was launched as a series of events in private venues in 2005, and it continues annually. But many highly publicized and visible events drew official attention and rebuke. For instance, permits were denied for the gay circuit party "Nation" in 2004, for various public talks relating to gay and lesbian rights, and for a "Pink Picnic" that was to be held in Singapore's botanic gardens in 2007. In all of these instances, and more, police stated that the granting of permits would be "contrary to the national interests." The Registrar of Societies gave the same reason when it refused the second attempt by LGBT organization People Like Us for registration as an official society in 2007. Furthermore, censorship restrictions on homosexual content in film, television, and theater were in many cases loosened but by no means dropped.

Limits were most directly and dramatically tested in 2007, when activists launched a lobbying campaign to repeal a colonial-era sodomy law. The campaign was undertaken as Singapore's Penal Code underwent a comprehensive review to bring it "up to date and make it more effective in maintaining a safe and secure society in today's context." As part of the reform, Section 377, prohibiting "carnal intercourse against the order of nature," was repealed so that "anal and oral sex, if done in private between a consenting adult heterosexual couple aged 16 years old and above" would no longer be criminalized (Singapore Ministry of Home Affairs 2006).[8] But Section 377A, prohibiting "gross indecency" between men, was left intact.[9] At this point, current PM Lee Hsien Loong stepped fully into the fray. In response to the presentation of two petitions to Parliament, one that called for the statute's repeal and the other that called for its retention, he delivered a dedicated speech on the issue: "They too must have a place in this society, and they too are entitled to their private lives. We should not make it harder than it already is for them to grow up and to live in a society where they are different from most Singaporeans. And we also do not want them to leave Singapore to go to more congenial places to live. But homosexuals should not set the tone for Singapore society" (Lee 2007). In the same speech, he further states,

> Homosexuals work in all sectors, all over the economy, in the public sector and in the civil service as well. They are free to lead their lives, free to pursue their social activities. But there are restraints and we do not approve of them actively promoting their lifestyles to others, or setting the tone for mainstream society. They live their lives. That is their personal life, it is their space. But the tone of the overall society, I think remains conventional, it remains straight, and we want it to remain so.

Thus Lee distanced the government from the anti-gay arguments made by those in the pro-retention camp by stating that the government does not "harass gays" or "act as moral policeman" and that it would not "proactively enforce Section 377A on them." Yet the statute stands as Lee affirmed that Singapore society is "still conservative" and fundamentally "straight."[10]

All government statements made on "the gay issue" since this 2007 speech have been consistent with it, and the Singapore Supreme Court rejected two constitutional challenges against Section 377A in November 2014. So the city-state's creative city project rolls on with a rhetorical commitment to tolerate sexual minorities but nothing more.[11] Full citizenship remains the preserve of Singapore's heterosexual subjects, while the LGBT community and its allies figure out what to do next. In this camp, there is certainly much frustration that LGBTs continue to live their lives on the margins in the city-state. There is also resentment over what Eng-Beng Lim has described as "the state's new—if volatile—attitude toward its queer citizenry: we'll leave you alone so long as homosexuality is not encouraged and is no more than a marketplace commodity" (Lim 2005b, 297–298). But there is simultaneously a sense of accomplishment. On the heels of the retention of Section 377A, journalist Janadas Devan (2007) stated, "I did not like one bit the upshot of the Prime Minister's speech—that 377A will stay because the majority, especially Christians and Muslims, are opposed to its scrubbing. But I was proud of what he had to say, and how he said it." Also, prominent activist Alex Au characterized the unsuccessful repeal campaign as one of "huge gains," noting that PM Lee, in his speech to Parliament, "spent time demolishing some of the arguments of the anti-gay side, thereby distancing his government from their agenda." He continued,

> Look closely, feel the vibes in society, and you'll see we achieved a lot. Countless straight men and women stood up to be counted, some making even better arguments in their blogs and speeches than gays themselves. Three ruling party MPs spoke up for repeal when previously, we all assumed the People's Action Party was monolithic on this question. Thousands of ordinary Singaporeans, faced with the headlines, have had an opportunity to think about the issue and clarify their thoughts on it.[12]

Despite the maintenance of the status quo in legislative and policy terms, there has certainly been much change since Lee Kuan Yew's first lukewarm public statement about gay Singaporeans in 1998.

Furthermore, the shift in official rhetoric has enabled the consolidation of an LGBT movement in the city-state. In this new, kinder, gentler environment in which the "promotion" of gay and lesbian "lifestyles" is nonetheless discouraged, Pink Dot, IndigNation, and many other organizations and initiatives have quickly emerged alongside the few longer standing groups like People Like Us. Gay activists have definitely found their feet, and they contribute to efforts to foster civil society and push for the liberalization of Singapore politics (see Chua 2015; Tan and Jin 2007). These many and varied efforts now make a claim on the social and cultural space that rather suddenly opened up for sexual minorities in the 2000s while making a careful plea for equity on the basis of sexual orientation. In the case of Pink Dot, the press release announcing the first event in 2009, boldly titled "Singaporeans to Make a Stand Against Prejudice and Bigotry," highlighted "discordant laws and policies" that force LGBT Singaporeans to live "secret lives" and then launched a sweeping appeal for "open-mindedness and understanding" in pursuit of "the freedom to love." Its organizers pitched the event as neither a protest nor a parade: "Pink Dot Sg is a non-profit movement started by a group of individuals who care deeply about the place that LGBT Singaporeans call home. Pink because it's a blend of red and white—the colour of Singapore's national flag. Also, it is the colour of our national identification cards. More importantly, Pink Dot Sg stands for a Singapore in which all Singaporeans, regardless of their sexual orientation, are free to love and be loved." This agenda has remained unchanged. Pink Dot works toward a Singapore "in which all Singaporeans are free to love and be loved."[13] It is "a symbol of Singapore's more inclusive future."[14] Thus LGBT activists mobilize to try to bring a gay-friendlier future into being.

Other critical scholars have told similar versions of this story about the changing place of homosexuality in Singapore in recent years, and some have offered conjecture on the prospects for the achievement of more thoroughgoing change for LGBTs in the city-state. In general, the present impasse is understood to be the result of a contradiction between the "traditional" "Asian" values to which the government clings in order to continue to assert its moral authority and maintain stability, and pragmatic economic concerns that require a more "cosmopolitan" outlook. If Singapore's government is indeed serious about opening up and fostering a creative, diverse city-state that stays ahead of the game, one common line of thinking proceeds, change will follow. For instance, Chris Tan asserts, "The state knows that it must cosmopolitanize, but the embracing of difference contradicts the sexual exclusivity inherent within normative notions of citizenship. The resolution of this contradiction presents an important challenge that Singapore has to face in the future" (Tan 2009, 150). Similarly, Meredith Weiss argues,

> The coupling of economic motivations for pluralist tolerance (specifically, per Richard Florida, toward gays and lesbians) and heightened conscientization and mobilization among queer Singaporeans seems likely to . . . favor . . . tangible improvements for the GLBT community. . . . Singapore's government may increasingly find that maintaining the discourses, norms, and policies apropos an attachment to the cultural relativism of "Asian values" appears increasingly incompatible with the nation-state's cosmopolitan economic dreams. (Weiss 2005, 288)

Thus various activists and critical commentators alike hold out hope for "progress" in a purportedly liberalizing Singapore.

On whether or when social justice for sexual minorities will follow as Singapore's government continues to balance its social and economic priorities, unfortunately I have no unique insight to offer. Instead, I turn now to argue for the need to advance another sort of counterdiscourse. In the next section, I provide further analysis of the events I have described here, taking seriously the government's unusual willingness to "stay behind" on the gay issue.

Staying Behind

Critical commentary highlighting the apparent contradiction between Singapore's cosmopolitan aspirations and its continuing discrimination against sexual minorities may very well be onto something. Activist strategies based on arguments that LGBT people deserve the "freedom to love" because they are Singaporeans first and foremost, and because they want to be able to contribute to the nation's progress and development, may—indeed, hopefully will—eventually bring results. But no matter how things turn out on this front, it is worth looking closely at the government's justifications for maintaining Singapore as a "straight space" while tolerating, but only tolerating, sexual minorities. Activists and other critics of the PAP's stance on homosexuality have by now well aired the position that Singapore will "fall behind" if it maintains its discriminatory stance. Alex Au, in an article arguing for gay marriage for Singaporeans, puts this plainly: "Singapore has to keep ourselves an attractive place for wealth and talent. We are already handicapped because countries like China, India, Thailand and others have huge domestic markets and low-cost resources. To compensate, we have to make our physical, legal, social and cultural environment— in addition to the economic—more attractive than theirs. We can't just keep pace. We have to be ahead of the pack."[15] Au, an outspoken critic of Singapore's progress narrative on a number of fronts, obviously advances this position as a strategic alignment with the values of competitiveness and success that the PAP government holds dear. Consider the striking similarities between Au's declaration and the following statement made by Goh Chok Tong, in his capacity as senior minister, just a few years later:

> We are on the right track to become a truly global city. . . . However, it is very much a work in progress and there is no room for complacency. Many other cities in Asia and the Middle East are vying to catch up with and overtake us. They are investing billions to make themselves attractive. Even well-established cities are reinventing themselves. We have to continue to learn from them and other vibrant cities, and reinvent ourselves to stay relevant and ahead of the competition. (Goh 2007)

The major difference between these two statements, however, is that Goh was not talking about LGBT rights.

In Singapore government discourse on the "gay issue," the language of "staying ahead" is strikingly absent. Au wrote the words above because this so thoroughly adaptable, rational, forward-looking government has instead explicitly chosen to "stay behind" on the issue of gay and lesbian rights. PM Lee Hsien Loong made this clear during his parliamentary address on the retention of Section 377A in 2007, in which he states, "When it comes to issues like the economy, technology, education, we better stay ahead of the game, watch where people are moving and adapt faster than others, ahead of the curve, leading the pack. And when necessary in such issues, we will move even if the issue is unpopular or controversial. . . . On issues of moral values with consequences to the wider society, first we should also decide what is right for ourselves. . . . So, we will let others take the lead, we will stay one step behind the front line of change" (Lee 2007). This is no trivial assertion, especially since, as intimated by PM Lee here, the Singapore government has indeed been very willing to move on certain controversial issues with significant societal implications for the sake of the health of the creative economy. Notably, it went ahead with plans to develop two prominent downtown "world-class resort and casino" complexes despite very strong and unusually vocal opposition from civic and religious groups in 2004 (see *Straits Times* 2004a, 2004b). It has also moved forward with aggressive recruitment of immigrants to expand Singapore's population base in the face of declining fertility rates, again despite considerable social pushback (see chapter 4). So, there is something in particular about the LGBT issue that causes Singapore government officials to fear that moving forward on rights provisions for this group will arrest development. Tracing PM Lee's argument further, this particular something becomes clear. He affirms, "The family is the basic building block of our society. It has been so and, by policy, we have reinforced this and we want to keep it so. And by 'family' in Singapore, we mean one man one woman, marrying, having children and bringing up children within that framework of a stable family unit" (Lee 2007). Not insignificantly, other major issues on which the Singapore government has chosen to "stay behind" also relate to the governance of familial, reproductive life. For instance, activist calls for better employment conditions for foreign workers go largely unheeded, as do calls for public provision of day care and more generous maternity leave policies that would make childbirth and child-raising more affordable and just generally easier for those below middle- to upper-income brackets. Who gets to reproduce Singapore's future, in a literal sense, is very much on the minds of PAP decision makers, and the "gay issue" is read through this preoccupation in key ways.

Of course, critical scholarship on sexual politics in Singapore has long highlighted the link between "family values" and discrimination against LGBT people. For instance, Laurence Wai-Teng Leong notes that "heterosexuality and the nuclear family are privileged by the state" (1995, 18); Kenneth Paul Tan states that homosexuality has been cast as a "threat to the traditional Asian family, which has been held up as the basic unit of Singaporean society" (Tan and Jin 2007, 185); and Meredith Weiss suggests that the "institution of the family" is "framed as necessary to Singapore's well-being and national survival, particularly to sustain a sense of local identity and moral standards as Singapore casts its lot as a global node" (Weiss 2005, 285). Furthermore, many local LGBT organizations, having likewise identified this stumbling block, have responded to the assertion that homosexuality is a threat to "family values" by very explicitly casting the gay and lesbian agenda as family friendly. In a 2006 press release, People Like Us stated that the maintenance of the sodomy law "damages family and public life by encouraging deception and dishonesty when people try to avoid discrimination and social or family conflict" and "creates pressure to emigrate, thus . . . splitting families when we say at the same time that stable and supportive families should be the bedrock of our society."[16] Pink Dot, as noted above, also frames its mission as one of helping gays and lesbians to fit into the national family, figuratively as well as literally. Among Singapore's pro-gay faction, such positions exemplify a frequent refrain that responds to the assertion that gays and lesbians are disenfranchised to protect the heterosexual family by imploring that they are not a threat to that norm and can and ought to be integrated within it.

Scholarly and activist responses to Singapore's exclusionary mode of sexual citizenship to date have therefore been largely trained on seizing the shift in government discourse to create new opportunities to fit in to the national family. This is a commonsense and strategic position. But it is also critically limited, as detailed in two recent groundbreaking works on Singapore LGBT politics— Lynette Chua's (2015) *Mobilizing Gay Singapore: Rights and Resistance in an Authoritarian State* and the edited collection *Queer Singapore: Illiberal Citizenship and Mediated Cultures* (Yue and Zubillaga-Pow 2012).

The former is the only book-length treatment of the history of Singapore's LGBT movement, tracing its existence from an early secretive bar culture in the 1970s, through private meetings in individual activists' living rooms in the early 1990s, and to the open, public resistance of the last decade. Chua coins the term "pragmatic resistance" to frame her analysis: "Under . . . authoritarian conditions, gay activists in Singapore learn to be creative as they find alternative ways to advance their movement while ensuring its survival. Even though they aspire toward legal reform and greater protection of their rights, they often do not deploy strategies and tactics familiar to activists in liberal democracies, especially street demonstrations. The result is a strategy of pragmatic resistance" (Chua 2015, 5). She provides an excellent account of the legal restrictions on collective mobilization and civil liberties in Singapore that effectively hamstring LGBT organizing, and indeed all other social movements in the city-state. She details severe legal obstacles to public assemblies and associations, limits to freedom of speech through the use of the Sedition Act and Internal Security Act and media licensing and management systems, and the conversion of single-member constituencies into group representation constituencies, which makes political turnover in individual districts difficult to achieve and helps the PAP maintain a firm grip on electoral politics. Furthermore, Chua highlights political norms that affect social movement organizing in Singapore, such as the principle of nonconfrontation, emphasis on the preservation of social stability, and the state's use of legal means to suppress and control dissent. Taken together, the legal and political environment in Singapore, she shows, is geared toward the preservation of the status quo, as "basic civil-political liberties are seen as trade-offs for engineering [a] particular vision of social stability and its fruits of economic progress" (Chua 2015, 34). In this climate in which asking for rights is nonconformist behavior and activist organizations face real threats of censure and disbandment, she shows how LGBT activists have learned to "toe the line as they push the boundaries" in order to make impressive inroads (Chua 2015, 44).

The collection *Queer Singapore*, edited by Audrey Yue and Jun Zubillaga-Pow, also grapples with the specificities of LGBT culture and politics in Singapore. It analyzes the emergence of LGBT activism and culture in a political context they call "illiberal pragmatism," a milieu that "facilitates state regulation of social identity while also creating new subjectivities for the new neoliberal economy" (Yue 2012, 2). Like Chua, the editors and contributors admire the "tactics of negotiation" that have led to the building of a vibrant LGBT movement and

subculture in the city-state "against a contradictory backdrop of sexual repression and cultural liberalization" (Yue 2012, 1). They also examine the negotiation
that Chua calls toeing the line while pushing boundaries, as the chapters "explore how local LGBT communities have thrived underground and above ground
through pragmatic modes of resistance and complicity" (Yue 2012, 25). They
dwell, in other words, on the ways in which activist and community groups
struggle against a regulatory state apparatus while they are inextricably intertwined within the new neoliberal economy. Overall, the contributors show "how
contemporary queer Singapore has emerged as a self-aware, action-oriented and
entrepreneurial culture that has worked within and twisted the illiberal logic of
State control," and thus the collection takes on a justifiably optimistic tone (Yue
2012, 25). But Yue's caution that the emergent queer public culture is caught up
in "the country's irrational and ambivalent modes of governance" is nonetheless
extremely significant as it forces us to be cognizant of the broader social forces
within which LGBT struggles are bound up (Yue 2012, 9).

The predominant trend within LGBT Singapore to build on the gains made
within the realm of cultural citizenship to subtly push for tangible political gains
for sexual minorities may eventually pay off. This would be an extraordinary
accomplishment. But shifting the notion of the national family to encompass
both heterosexuals *and* homosexuals will make little dent in the heteronormative logics that cultivate the narrow family norms underpinning socially unjust
notions of development. In Singapore, as everywhere else, heteronormativity
and notions of the proper national family are complex, deeply rooted, and tied
to a range of structural forces such as patriarchy, racism, capitalism, ableism,
and more. They thus cannot be countered solely through appeals for LGBT inclusion. Again, the identity-based, assimilationist stance adopted by many local
LGBT organizations makes much sense. These organizations exist precariously
in the slightly liberalized but still illiberal city-state, and their actions are highly
circumscribed since the shadow of the still strong state is a long one.[17] But here
I do not face those constraints and can begin to at least imagine a different sort
of queer political challenge to Singapore's exclusionary sexual citizenship and
intimate governance regimes. As Chua notes, "In authoritarian Singapore, to
speak out is to mount the first act of resistance" (2015, 5). So I want to push
the conversation on sexual politics in Singapore to address not just hegemonic
heterosexuality but hegemonic heteronormativity, even though activists and
local commentators cannot afford to advance such a broad-based critique at
this juncture.

We know that Singapore's gays and lesbians are disenfranchised to protect
"the family." Multiple government officials have clearly and repeatedly made this
clear. But what has been strikingly absent from discussions of "family values"
in the context of debates over the place of homosexuality in the city-state is the
fact that "the family" and "heterosexuality" are terms that do not map neatly or

completely onto each other. What has not yet been discussed, because doing so is too politically risky, is the fact that "the family" that Singapore's government seeks to protect regulates sexuality, and much else, along more than the heterosexual-homosexual divide. In my reading of PM Lee's 2007 speech, he tacitly suggests as much. Rather than dismissing the concerns of LGBT people by denouncing homosexuality outright as a threat to some sort of universal heterosexual moral framework, Lee took pains to clarify that the gay and lesbian community "include[s] people who are responsible and valuable, highly respected contributing members of society." On the basis that "among them are some of our friends, our relatives, our colleagues, our brothers and sisters, or some of our children," Lee saw fit to prescribe that "they too must have a place in this society, and they too are entitled to their private lives." But while he downplayed fears of homosexuality per se and strongly encouraged Singaporeans to adopt a "live and let attitude" toward gays and lesbians, Lee also insisted that "homosexuals should not set the tone for society." He insisted that "the overall society . . . remains conventional, it remains straight," and he did this for the very specific reason that "the family is the basic building block of our society" (Lee 2007). In other words, PM Lee complicated the polarizing heterosexuality-homosexuality binary by asserting that queerness is not a threat to heterosexuality per se, but a threat to a specific heterosexual family norm. The contest does not, in other words, entail simply a struggle for dominance between sexual identities but involves the maintenance of heteronormativity. It is therefore necessary to go beyond the heterosexuality-homosexuality issue that has so far dominated public debate over sexual citizenship in the city-state to examine the cultural politics of intimacy in global city Singapore.

Beyond Limits

LGBT movements have gained unprecedented traction in many sites around the globe. As human rights protections for sexual minorities have been achieved in numerous (though by no means most) countries and the purported economic benefits of gay-friendliness have appealed to some urban and national boosters, LGBT persons are now at least tolerated in a range of sites, including Singapore. The city-state's long-standing PAP government has slightly altered its mode of rule in its era of creative urbanism, and as it allows for more public participation while still expending much effort to maintain social control, a new governmental rhetoric of limited openness toward sexual minorities has led to unprecedented public debates on the place of homosexuality in the city-state and enabled the growth of a nascent LGBT movement. But tolerance for the sake of attracting and retaining "talent" has not disrupted the teleological and fundamentally heteronormative logics of progress and social reproduction that guided Singapore's transformation from "third world to first" (Lee 2000). Singapore is still a "straight space," as PM Lee asserts, in that full citizenship is the preserve of heterosexual subjects. Some LGBT persons, those whose activities contribute to the new economy, can step tentatively into the public sphere (at least for as long as they are seen to be creating value), but enfranchisement is off the table as the state is wary of fundamental social and cultural change. LGBTs may have a role to play in the productive sphere, the state allows, but their public and private lives remain curtailed to keep them out of the sphere of social reproduction, out of the sphere of that "basic building block" of Singapore society, the family.

Pink Dot and other activist organizations and critical commentators have responded to this government position by staking a claim for more space in the city-state while hoping for and working toward a more inclusive future for LGBT Singaporeans. Yet, considering the economically forward-looking PAP government's willingness to "stay behind" on LGBT rights and other social issues, it is apparent that the terrain is much more complicated than the dominant focus in Singapore public discourse on a heterosexual-homosexual dividing line suggests. The government's position is clear. The nation's future depends not just on sound economic policies but also on sound population policies, and this project involves more than the preservation of a heterosexual norm in the city-state. It involves the preservation of a specific notion of "the family," one that excludes many more than sexual minorities. To envision and enable a socially just global city future, therefore, the debate must be pried further open. Critical responses might venture well beyond arguments for LGBT equality to advance a more extensive political challenge to the logic of reproductive futurism that underpins Singapore's urban and national developmental strategies. For while the establishment of heteronormativity as a central aspect of Singapore's colonial and postcolonial modernization projects has produced sexual exclusion to be sure, it has also and inextricably constructed an intimate sphere bound up with a relentless progress narrative that has implications for the workings of citizenship along lines of race, class, gender, and nationality. As Carla Freccero argues, a queer approach that goes beyond single-issue identity politics requires that we think "'queer' as a critique of (temporal) normativity tout court rather than sexual normativity specifically" (2007, 489).

On queerness and temporality, Lee Edelman's *No Future: Queer Theory and the Death Drive* (2004) is perhaps the best known text. In a provocative Lacanian analysis, Edelman challenges the logic of "reproductive futurism," at the center of which he locates the figure of the Child. Edelman declares that for a queer ethic to be truly oppositional it must refuse the embrace of acceptance via participation in circuits of kinship and reproduction; it must disavow the future. He declares the "proper task" of queer theory to be "the ceaseless disappropriation of every propriety" (2004, 24), and thus, for him, "*queerness* names the side of those *not* 'fighting for the children,' the side outside the consensus by which all politics confirms the absolute value of reproductive futurism" (2004, 3, emphasis original). Notably, it has also attracted much critique. For instance, José Muñoz's analysis in *Cruising Utopia: The Then and There of Queer Futurity* (2009) begins from a similar starting point to Edelman's—that is, the dominance of reproductive futurism and the political impoverishment of a countermovement framed narrowly around the demand for same-sex marriage. Though inspired by the polemic of *No Future*, he forcefully writes against its antisocial, antirelational political proposition. Muñoz, rather than disavowing the future, advocates its utopian recasting. Forgetting the future, Muñoz argues, is not a political option since only a very privileged few can afford to do so. Edelman, as he writes against what he identifies as a universal politics of reproductive futurism, invokes a universal "queer" subject. But as Muñoz states, "imagining a queer subject who is abstracted from the sensuous intersectionalities that mark our experience is an ineffectual way out" (2009, 96). "Queer" subjects are multiple and are differently positioned in relation to the dominant heteronormative order along lines of race, class, gender, and more. They cannot, in all their variability, simply opt out. We must therefore reenvision (see also Smith 2010; Winnubst 2010).

To envision alternative futures for Singapore, I suggest that we must look back. To understand how we got to this era in which LGBT persons are tolerated in the "straight space" of Singapore, and to chart ways of achieving social transformation, how the heteronormative logic came to take root in the city-state must be excavated. The next two chapters dwell in good measure on Singapore's late colonial and early postcolonial years, as I argue that this is the period to which we must look to gain a fuller understanding of the present-day government's stubbornness to do any more than tolerate sexual difference, and to shed light on the ways in which recent debates about sexual citizenship in the city-state are connected to a much wider array of issues than has been widely acknowledged to date. They move out from the debates on homosexuality versus heterosexuality that have been so well aired in Singapore to instead grapple with the politics of intimacy in the city-state, especially highlighting the family's function as a regulative governing fiction in colonial and postcolonial Singapore, and detailing the ways in which a "proper family" norm has been carefully cultivated throughout its history. Through analysis of deployments of family, housing, and migration policies, the next chapters demonstrate this norm's role in producing both a stable population of "quality" citizens as well as multiple "queered" others who fall outside the very particular heterosexual family norm upon which Singapore's developmental aims have come to rest.

CHAPTER 3

Section 377A and the Colonial Trace

Section 377A of the Singapore Penal Code, a colonial-era statute prohibiting "gross indecency" between two men, has been a focal point of the debates around the place of homosexuality in the city-state.[1] When the Ministry of Home Affairs undertook a reform of the Penal Code in 2007, activists boldly seized the opportunity to try to push the government down a path to a future of LGBT inclusion and acceptance by calling for this statute's repeal. Many arguments were mobilized by campaigners on the pro-repeal side, including calls for pluralism and democratic values, appeals for fairness, equity, and nondiscrimination, assertions of the right to privacy and individual autonomy, and critiques of the legislation as unconstitutional, or at least as a "bad law" that protects against no demonstrable harm and is largely unenforced. In this chapter, I begin to examine the politics of reproductive futurism on which Singapore's urban and national development project relies by departing from one particularly popular line of argument in the debates that ensued in the mainstream press, online forums, and in parliament: that is, that Section 377A, as a colonial leftover, is an anachronism in contemporary Singapore. As the reform exercise explicitly aimed to bring the Penal Code "up to date and make it more effective in maintaining a safe and secure society in today's context," many activists and critical commentators highlighted its status as a British import and labeled it both out of time and out of place in the modern city-state (Singapore Ministry of Home Affairs 2006). While a common argument on the retention side of the debate cited the need to uphold Section 377A as an expression of "Asian values," others countered that the statute is a "reflection of the sentiments of the British colonial masters" and is thus "not even Asian in origin."[2] The British themselves, it was frequently noted, have since removed the original statute and liberalized their sexual offense laws (see Cheah 2007). In any case, many argued, laws reflecting colonial norms and values have no place in postcolonial Singapore.[3]

In his speech detailing the city-state government's official rationale for the decision to retain Section 377A, Prime Minister Lee Hsien Loong specifically addressed this colonial throwback argument:

> We are not starting from a blank slate, trying to design an ideal arrangement; neither are we proposing new laws against homosexuality. We have what we have inherited and what we have adapted to our circumstances. . . . We inherited section 377A from the British, imported from English Victorian law—Victorian from the period of Queen Victoria in the 19th century—via the Indian Penal Code, via the Straits Settlements Penal Code, into Singapore law. Asian societies do not have such laws, not in Japan, China and Taiwan. But it is part of our landscape. We have retained it over the years. So, the question is: what do we want to do about it now? Do we want to do anything about it now? If we retain it, we are not enforcing it proactively. Nobody has argued for it to be enforced very vigorously in this House. If we abolish it, we may be sending the wrong signal that our stance has changed, and the rules have shifted. (Lee 2007)

In the same speech, PM Lee further asserts that the family is a "basic building block" of Singapore society because "by policy, we have reinforced this and we want to keep it so." He notes, "If we look at the way our Housing and Development Board flats are, our neighbourhoods, our new towns, they are, by and large, the way Singaporeans live. It is not so in other countries, particularly in the West, anymore, but it is here" (Lee 2007). PM Lee thus set out a rather different notion of the relationship between the past and the present, the colonial and the postcolonial, than did the pro-repeal campaigners. He and his government acknowledge Section 377A's colonial provenance. But they do not interpret the statute's origins to present a postcolonial paradox. Instead, they maintain that this colonial-era sexual regulation has been retained because it is indeed contemporary and local. It has been retained because present-day Singapore is a place in time in which the rules have not shifted.

However unwittingly, PM Lee's dismissal of the argument that being postcolonial entails an outright rejection of the remnants of a colonial past is not out of step with postcolonial theory's claim that the postcolonial condition is not beyond the colonial. In this chapter, I pick up on this line of argument to frame a critical response to this illiberal sexual politics. By following the assertion that Singapore's past valuably shapes its present, I demonstrate that Section 377A is by no means simply an anachronistic leftover and that consideration of heteronormativity as a colonial trace is necessary to better understand the politics of its perpetuation. I first briefly discuss some scholarship on the sexual politics of empire, work that foregrounds the central role that the regulation of sexuality played in the colonizer-colonized relationship and goes some way toward advancing both a queer critique of the colonial condition and a postcolonial analysis of sexual politics. I then argue that to adequately examine sexual politics in the postcolony, it is necessary to extend the dominant focus in the literature on sexuality and colonialism to encompass the transition to postcolonial governance. To understand why PM Lee proclaims that Section 377A is rightfully in place in contemporary Singapore, I read the history of sexuality in the colony in a way that takes seriously the role played not just by the colonizers but also by the colonized elite in shaping a proper intimate sphere as a foundation for "development."

Putting this postcolonial queer approach to work, the remainder of the chapter delves into archival records from Singapore's late colonial period. It thus begins to detail a history of the regulation of intimacy in the city-state that the next chapter, which deals mainly with the postcolonial period, carries forward. Although scant mention of homosexuality or of the passage of Section 377A is made in the public record, the archive is rich with evidence of urgent efforts by both the colonizers and the colonized elite to reign in deviant heterosexualities and facilitate family formation in order to delineate a proper domestic sphere. The finding that the "homosexual" is but one of the "perverse" figures deemed to be an obstacle to the creation of the "quality" population required for Singapore's future growth and development further supports this book's central argument that the heteronormative logic underpinning the regulation of sexuality in Singapore necessitates a critical response that goes far beyond championing the rights of sexual minorities to scrutinize the myriad injustices that accompany the post/colonial politics of reproductive futurism in the contemporary city-state.

A History of Sexuality

As already discussed, much queer scholarship productively eschews a literal sexual referent and enforces the point that homophobia and heterosexism—and indeed all modes of sexual regulation—must be interpreted in the context of broad sets of power relations. Thus an interdisciplinary body of work examines how sexual norms and discourses are unavoidably intertwined with geopolitics, colonialisms, and nationalisms. This work goes beyond sexual identity per se to explore the ways in which sexual norms exist in a relationship of mutual constitution with racialized, gendered, and class processes. It also takes us beyond a narrow focus on the prohibition of or permission for specific sexual acts and identities to attend to the public construction of an intimate sphere. However, as Anjali Arondekar has pointed out, though informed by postcolonial thought, much of this "work focuses overwhelmingly on contemporary issues with colonialism appearing more as a referent than a sustained period of study" (2005, 12n6). So it is worth briefly discussing some literature that engages in explicit historical excavations of the confluence of gender, race, sexuality, and empire.

The British Empire, of which Singapore was a part, has been particularly well explored in this regard by scholars such as Anne McClintock (1995), Lenore Manderson (1996), Philip Howell (2009), and Richard Phillips (2006). Additionally, Ann Stoler (2002, 1995) has provided immensely productive insights on the intimate politics of the colonial Dutch East Indies. A common aim across this work is the disruption of depictions of colonial power relations as somehow stable, fixed, and imposed from without. The colonized-colonizer binary is deconstructed to enable analysis of colonial hegemony as the product of constant contest over meanings, ideologies, and notions of identity. For these scholars, colonial culture is characterized by dynamism, structure does not overdetermine agency, and boundaries are porous. Perceptions of the distance between metropole and periphery are challenged by readings that attend to the many relations between these sites. This work interrogates colonial power to demonstrate that "there was no such thing as a 'home base' of British sexuality" (Howell 2000, 336). It calls attention to the "productivity of the margins" in the establishment of the bourgeois sexuality of the "centre" (Phillips 2006, 163). These are exceedingly useful insights, and much of what follows in this chapter takes them up to examine the ways in which the colonial administration sought to enact population reform in the late colonial period through the creation of certain family norms. But there is, nonetheless, one shortcoming that needs to be addressed for my purposes. Even these postcolonial examinations of sexuality that deal concertedly with the specific histories and geographies of colonialism take us only a limited way toward understanding the legacy of colonial regulation in postcolonies because although the center is thrown off its axis in this work, attention is still drawn inevitably back to Europe. The crucial undertaking of destabilizing monolithic caricatures of colonial power leads productively to insightful analyses of the constitution of the colonizer. Given this emphasis, the agency of the colonized, though acknowledged, is not the focal point of study. This is a significant gap since the objects of colonial rule eventually became postcolonial governors, who are key actors in the contemporary regulation of sexuality in the era of independence.

Thus, while the specificities of modes of colonial governance are the main object of study for scholars seeking to understand colonial sexual politics and the broader construction of intimacy of which they are part, a light must be shone on the transition to postcolonial governance when analyzing postcolonial sexual and intimate politics. Since the post/colony itself can usefully be more firmly located at the center of study, this chapter extends the insights of histories of the colonial regulation of sexuality to explore the postcolonial regulation of intimacy and its local antecedents. It builds on acknowledgments of the "tensions of empire" (see Cooper and Stoler 1997) that have enriched understanding of the colonial situation by attending to the roles of both colonial administrators and certain colonized actors in shaping sexual norms during Singapore's late colonial period.[4] I highlight the role of the latter group since the subsequent ascendance of these actors to positions of power after independence has played an important part in narrowing the imagination of intimate possibilities in contemporary Singapore.

In Singapore, the colonizer-colonized distinction was certainly a core element in the production of colonial power relations that were fundamentally divisive. The status of the full modern citizen was reserved by the British administration for those hailing from Europe, the purported center of civilization. The colonized were associated by that same administration with tradition or custom and generally treated as objects of rule. But to understand both the colonial and postcolonial projects, the stratification of the colonized and the fact that a completely discrete colonized-colonizer binary was more fiction than fact must not be overlooked. The British administration relied on segments of that population to act as interpreters, cultural informants, and liaisons with various groups. In addition, business ties, property ownership, and educational attainments were elevators of status and created a colonized elite. Crucially, many members of this colonized elite by no means desired to throw off the mantle of modernity. Rather, they passionately argued for their rightful place within it. In the Straits Settlements, as Philip Holden notes, "various non-European communities attempted to represent themselves as modern subjects in the Anglophone public sphere" since the end of the nineteenth century (1999, 59). Initiatives along these lines from members of the Tamil and Eurasian communities have been well documented, while, as Holden and others point out, members of the Chinese community "made the most determined effort." As he states, "Through a strategic reinscription of Confucianism as the embodiment of reason, the body project of the Straits Chinese attempted to move Europe aside, and produce new Asian subjects who were the natural heirs of the Enlightenment" (Holden 1999, 59).[5]

As discussed in more detail below, certain colonized elites became "active enunciators of the colonial discourse" (Yao 1999, 117). To acknowledge this colonial complicity, however, is not to suggest that colonial elites grafted themselves wholesale onto the colonial project. Such a move was neither possible nor desirable. The British colonial administration appreciated the efforts of members of the colonized elite to uplift and enlighten the various colonized communities over which they ruled. But the administration did not read these efforts as expressions of an authentic European modernity but viewed them as attempts at modernity born of mimicry. Thus, the colonized elite, though a valuable aid to the colonial project, could never fully assume its stewardship. At the same time, many members of the colonized elite loyally embraced their status as British subjects while being very much aware of its limits and calling frequent attention to the fundamental contradiction of British colonialism, that is, "its self-justification through the idea of trusteeship and tutelage, but its simultaneous refusal to grant equal status to colonial subjects who had passed through this tutelage" (Holden 1999, 66). The colonial state, as enacted in the Straits Settlements, could never be a fully representative polity. It could never foster a nation of subjects. Herein lies the obvious impetus for anticolonial struggle in the Straits Settlements. While the British administration introduced a project of colonial modernity, it could never fulfill its goals. For "the colonial state was necessarily incapable of fulfilling the criterion of representativeness—the fundamental condition that makes modern power a matter of interiorized self-discipline rather than external correction" (Partha Chatterjee, quoted in Holden 2003, 313). The postcolonial state, however, could fulfill this criterion of representativeness, and in Singapore, as elsewhere, "modern disciplinary power . . . would be perfected not by the colonialists but by the new nations that emerged from colonialism" (Holden 2003, 313).

With the achievement of independence from colonial rule, the new Singapore government embraced the idea of modernization wholeheartedly. Postcolonial Singapore, as C. J. Wee observes, has been shaped by a desire "to be even *more consistently modern* than the former colonial masters were" (2007, 20, emphasis original). Just as certain segments of the colonized community were important actors in the late colonial drive toward progress and development, they pushed forward an ambitious agenda for the improvement of the people of the postcolonial city-state. Singapore's postcolonial governance, in short, is the result of deep conversations with the ideas that drove colonial rule, conversations that have taken place both long before and long after that rule ended.[6] As such, to understand the present-day Singapore polity, colonial power relations cannot be consigned to the past since "colonial discourse is . . . not a nightmare that we should analyze upon waking, but rather a particular mode of power that forms the basis for other disciplinary projects in the present" (Holden 2003, 315). In this light, PM Lee's assertion that Section 377A has a place in contemporary Singapore precisely because it is a colonial holdover that has been adapted and purposefully retained over the postcolonial period makes much sense. It also presents a challenge for those seeking to critically respond to this law's persistence. If this colonial-era law is still relevant in postcolonial Singapore, then it is necessary to trace how and why this remnant from the colonial modernizing project haunts the present. It is necessary to consider the colonial roots of postcolonial sexual regulation in order to understand and respond to a postcolonial transition that yielded liberation without freedom. This chapter takes up this task.

To be clear, my aim in exploring Section 377A as a colonial trace is not to search for the ancestors of contemporary sexual minorities. It is not to find the origin of a contest between dominant "straight" and marginal "gay" identities. As Anjali Arondekar argues, sexualities scholarship ought to "question the dependence on a recovered history to sanction our surviving present" (2005, 16). Many scholars have gone on "an old-fashioned global hunt for the homosexual" (Arondekar 2005, 19), looking for hints of queer bodies and lives in other places and times in order to bolster claims to equity in the present. But while the impulse to recover the lost voices of gay (and less often lesbian, bisexual, or trans) progenitors is an understandable one, Arondekar questions whether sexual identities can be found in the archive at all (2005, 18).[7] She observes that historiographies of colonial sexuality tend to treat homosexuality as "both obvious and elusive—undeniable anecdotally (in colonial travelogues, ethnopornography, etc.), yet rarely substantiated in any official archival form." Such a treatment, she argues, merely reiterates the colonial logic of "native perversity" as "ontological excess" (2005, 19). In other words, it passes off objects as subjects. Chandan Reddy makes a similar point, stating that "the archive is not a passive domain in which differences . . . can be found, extracted, and restored to their fullness" (2005, 115). Instead of seeking to locate sexual others, therefore, he advocates that sexuality scholars treat the archive as "the active technique by which sexual, racial, gendered, and national differences, both historical and futural, are suppressed, frozen, and redirected as the occasion for a universal knowledge" (2005, 115).

In the remainder of this chapter, I narrate a history of sexuality in relation to the Singapore case that is consonant with the approaches of Arondekar and Reddy. I aim not to salvage a lost past of sexual difference, but to trace the notions of sexual propriety and impropriety that came to make sense in the post/colonial imaginary. My narrative is, in other words, a Foucauldian one. Along with Foucault in *The History of Sexuality, Volume 1*, I am fundamentally concerned with the power of normalization. In the book's last part, "The Right of Death and Power over Life," Foucault details his notion that "a normalizing society is the historical outcome of a technology of power centered on life" (1978, 144). He examines "biopower" as a "power over life" that centers on two poles—"the body as a machine" and "the species body"—and understands sex as a political issue tied both to the disciplines of the body and to the regulation of populations (1978, 139). Governance, as a "taking charge of life" (1978, 143) that renders "the action of the norm" exceedingly important, is likewise my critical target (1978, 144). I read Singapore's colonial archive not for evidence of a British clampdown on a presumably inherent sexual otherness, but for the emergence of modes of governing the intimate sphere in the service of modernization, for the emergence of a notion of reproductive futurism that has sustained contemporary reach. I turn now to Singapore's late colonial archives to detail a politics of population that haunts the present-day postcolony.

Population and the Postcolony

Commentators on both sides of Singapore's Section 377A repeal debates agree on at least the point that this sodomy law has a colonial provenance. Indeed, it was put into the Straits Settlements Penal Code by the British administration toward the tail end of its rule in 1938. Yet the archival record yields very little information about the law's specific colonial roots. Public commentary on Section 377A from the time of its enactment is scarce. When it was added to the Penal Code, its first reading was noted only briefly in the Legislative Council Proceedings. On its second reading, the attorney general made the following remarks:

> It is unfortunately the case that acts of the nature described have been brought to notice. As the law now stands, such acts can only be dealt with, if at all, under the Minor Offences Ordinance, and then only if committed in public. Punishment under the Ordinance is inadequate and the chances of detection are small. It is desired, therefore, to strengthen the law and to bring it into line with English Criminal Law, from which this clause is taken, and the law of various other parts of the Colonial Empire of which it is only necessary to mention Hong Kong and Gibraltar where conditions are somewhat similar to our own. (Straits Settlements 1938b, B49)

Beyond these statements, I did not find any reports of Section 377A's passage into law in local newspapers, in correspondence with the London Colonial Office, or in any of the numerous publications produced by and for members of the various colonized communities.

Prior to its passage, three Straits Settlements annual reports contain brief references to male prostitution as a problem. The 1936 report simply states that "male prostitution was also kept in check, as and when encountered" (Straits Settlements 1936, 856). The 1937 report goes slightly further: "Widespread existence of male prostitution was discovered and reported to the Government whose orders have been carried out. . . . Sodomy is a penal offence; its danger to adolescents is obvious; obvious too, is the danger of blackmail, the demoralizing effect on disciplined forces and on a mixed community which looks to the Government for wholesome governing" (Straits Settlements 1937, 835). The 1938 report states definitively that "male prostitution and other forms of beastliness were stamped out as and when opportunity occurred" (Straits Settlements 1938a, 414). Furthermore, there is oblique reference to seemingly relevant events in the memoirs of a colonial official, who states, "Nor should I fail to mention the social upheaval of the 'thirties when the diary of a professional Chinese catamite fell into the hands of the police, resulting in an official inquiry, the disgrace of several prominent persons, and the suicide of two of those who were implicated in the matter" (Purcell 1965, 250). From this scant evidence, I surmise that the colonial administration decided in 1938 to legislate same-sex sexual activity in order to stamp out male prostitution. But why exactly it took this step at this particular time is unknown. It is certainly not the case that colonial rulers were previously unaware of such practices. Although the archival record contains very little mention of same-sex sexual activity in the Straits Settlements, it was not off the radar. As Lenore Manderson notes, in frequent debates over the preponderance of female prostitutes in the settlement, colonial officials argued that prostitution ought not be outlawed because, in the words of one colonial representative, it was a "necessary evil, to save us from something worse" (1996, 167). Public officials thus pushed for attention to "the improvement of the physical conditions of brothel buildings and the health of the women who worked there" so that "intelligent Chinamen" would not "descend to forms of unnatural vice" rather than frequent unsanitary brothels (Manderson 1996, 167).[8] Furthermore, James Warren (2003) finds coroner reports of anal syphilis that attest to the colonial administration's knowledge of the existence of male same-sex sexual activity.

Given this paucity of evidence, if the focus of my effort to understand Section 377A as a colonial trace were trained narrowly on the goal of finding the "homosexual" within Singapore's colonial past, there would be little more to say. There are simply too few pointers in the archives to convey understanding of the ways in which male same-sex activity came to be regulated in colonial Singapore. On the basis of existing evidence, it is not possible to flesh out the common claim made by some of those on the pro-repeal side of the contemporary Section 377A debates that the British imposed their Victorian era Christian sexual morality on colonized populations who maintained no prohibitions on same-sex sexual activity. The archive contains insufficient material on the colonial administration's views on "homosexuality" as well as on the colonized communities' responses to its regulation to ground such an argument. But when we fan out from an understanding of Section 377A as prohibiting male same-sex sexual activity or outlawing "homosexuality" to take a view of this legislation as just one part of the formation of an expansive heteronormative regulatory framework, the archive overflows. When we look beyond the statute's literal sexual referent to instead explore the provenance of the ideal family that the postcolonial government seeks to protect by upholding this law, colonial traces abound in the public record.

In contemporary Singapore, Section 377A remains in force because the PAP government argues that homosexuality is a threat to the nuclear family norm. To be sure, this norm is firmly established, as PM Lee asserted when rejecting the 2007 repeal campaign. When Section 377A was enacted in 1938, however, Singapore society had a very different complexion. This now modern nation of settled families was then a colonial entrepôt mainly composed of single male migrant workers. In another major difference between the two time frames, while the PAP government seeks to sustain the contemporary demographic status quo, colonial officials and colonized elites had grown deeply dissatisfied with the city's makeup by the late colonial period and fundamental population reform efforts had gained considerable momentum by 1938. Otherwise stated, the transformation of this colonial entrepôt comprised of single male migrant workers into a modern nation of families was well underway by the time that Section 377A was deemed a necessary legislative addition. This sodomy law may perhaps have been passed out of an official desire to protect or reinforce the emergent family norm. Archival evidence to confirm or deny this contention is unfortunately lacking. But what can be demonstrated with available material is that Section 377A was definitely not the only means of intimate regulation deployed by the British colonial administration in the last decades of its rule. As PM Lee noted in his speech to Parliament in 2007, the family ideal that Section 377A has been upheld to protect in contemporary Singapore is certainly the product of much work. Existing scholarship already emphasizes the role of the postcolonial PAP government in promoting the family ideal as a foundation of Singapore's remarkable socioeconomic development, and I will engage with such scholarship in the next chapter. In the remainder of this section, I trace the beginnings of the work of inculcating a familial norm within Singapore society to the late colonial period. To do so, I draw on the considerable archival evidence of the formation of an expansive heteronormative framework during this period, a framework of which Section 377A is only one facet.[9] I argue that in order to understand the colonial provenance of heteronormativity in Singapore, we ought not focus narrowly on the passage of Section 377A. Instead, we ought to widen the purview of our analyses by examining the late colonial push toward development and modernization for the ways in which it centralized the establishment of heteronormality in place of "abnormal" population dynamics and "backward" cultural practices.

My argument proceeds in three parts. In the first section that follows, I look at the principle of noninterference with the intimate practices of the Straits Settlements inhabitants that characterized British colonial rule until around 1900, and how it gave way when colonial policies shifted from a narrow focus on production toward an approach that coupled emphasis on production with a new interest in social reproduction. Concerns with balancing the population's sex ratio and creating conditions to facilitate family life in the colony are detailed here. Furthermore, I highlight that this late colonial push for family formation and proper intimacy was not merely a British imposition, but a project that was endorsed by many within at least the elite strata of the colonized communities. Next, I turn to two cases that illustrate that although both groups—the colonial administrators and colonized elites—sought to transform Singapore's population into one of settled families, opinions varied on how such families should be governed. The second section that follows explores debates over Chinese marriages, while the third section considers the subtly different views of the British administration and certain colonized elites on the regulation of family in the context of housing policy. Through these cases, I show that both the colonial administration and the soon-to-be postcolonial governors played important roles in putting in place a notion of the "Singapore family" that has underpinned urban and national development efforts since the colony became an independent city-state. Furthermore, I emphasize that while the British colonial administration began to intervene in the intimate lives of the colonized in significant ways during the late colonial period, its manipulation of kinship forms was limited to the extent that it governed colonized families according to the "customs" of the colonized communities. But the colonized elite pushed against these limits and laid the foundations for the modern family that has been a central element of Singapore society in the postcolonial era. Based on this evidence, I argue that, along with Section 377A, the family norm that the PAP government seeks to protect in postcolonial Singapore is most certainly a colonial throwback. In addition, understanding its colonial trace makes apparent that heteronormativity in colonial and postcolonial Singapore has as much to do with racism, elitism, nationalism, and gender bias as it does with sexual identity.

Finding the Colonial Family

For much of its colonial history, Singapore's British governors focused squarely on production and spared little concern for social reproduction (see Manderson 1996). Wealth was extracted from this trading outpost through the labor of a majority population of single male migrants hailing from China, India, and elsewhere. As such, the colonial administration largely did not meddle in the intimate lives of the Straits Settlements' inhabitants and generally accepted that the combination of an "abnormal" sex ratio and the cultural "character" of the colonized population led to the formation of rather different social mores in this corner of the periphery than prevailed in the metropole. But colonial thinking began to change around 1900. To ensure prolonged profits, colonial administrators became convinced of the need to bridge the fiscal and the social in the form of concerted efforts at socioeconomic development, and as such, social reproduction came into view. Over the remainder of the colonial period, the British governors undertook a range of initiatives to balance the sex ratio and build a proper domestic sphere. Thus the family, as a tool for securing the perpetuation and prosperity of the polity, was found.[10] This section focuses on the late colonial administration's views on the settlement's population dynamics as a problem for development. It then discusses the ways in which these aims to alter colonized communities through population reform found resonance with dominant discourses of advancement, enlightenment, and uplift circulating among the colonized elites, within limits.

"It has always to be borne in mind that the population of Singapore is a peculiar one" (Simpson 1907, 2). This line, from a 1907 report on sanitary conditions in the settlement, expresses a prominent theme within Singapore's colonial discourse. Across censuses, annual reports, housing studies, legislative council proceedings, social hygiene treatises, and more, the "peculiar" or, as it is more frequently put in the archival record, "abnormal" population of Singapore is centrally featured when describing both the social conditions of the colony and its prospects for future growth. This characterization of colonial Singapore's population as unusual is pegged primarily to two factors—its highly imbalanced sex ratio and its migrant composition. As stated in the 1955 *Master Plan*, "Singapore originally possessed only a small indigenous population not at all interested in a wage economy, and received the immigrant labour force without reserve" (Singapore 1955b, 13). This statement's condescending tone toward the settlement's Malay community notwithstanding, it accurately conveys the impetus for the colonial administration's open approach to immigration that persisted into the twentieth century.[11] As the colony was populated by flows of mainly male migrants, a skewed sex ratio resulted. As late as 1911, there were eight men to every woman in the population as a whole and ten men to every woman in the colonized immigrant communities (Singapore 1955b, 16).[12] Notably, while mentions of Singapore's "abnormal" population within the colonial administration's public record reach well back into the colony's nineteenth-century history, this demographic situation was not narrated as particularly problematic until around the turn of the twentieth century. Prior to that time, it was instead largely seen as simply a reality that required management.[13] The shift in colonial thinking on Singapore's abnormal population from its depiction as a mere fact to be dealt with to a view that it was a serious impediment to the colony's development and growth that thus required fundamental response is illustrated most clearly in changes in the colonial administration's treatment of prostitution over time.

As noted above, female prostitutes were in good supply in colonial Singapore, and in frequent debates on this topic among those within the colonial establishment it was held that the provision of commercial sex was a "necessary evil, to save us from something worse" (Manderson 1996, 167). Beyond the specific desire to stem the spread of same-sex sexual activity, local colonial officials resisted entreaties from the colonial home office and other social reformers in the metropole to stamp out prostitution in large part because they held that the "sexual appetites" of the colonized population had to be filled. The majority view among Singapore's colonizers was that "natural" sexual urges required satisfaction in order to maintain social order in this overwhelmingly male environment. Furthermore, the local colonial establishment determined that "the Asiatic regards prostitution and sex generally on a different plane to that of an European."[14] These positions, that prostitution must be allowed in male-dominated Singapore and that moral stances on the issue ought to be understood as culturally relative, were firmly held by the local British colonial administration throughout its rule. Nonetheless, as I now turn to demonstrate, the centrality of the figure of the prostitute in colonial Singapore's landscape changed drastically over time as a commitment to population reform gradually took root. In short, despite the persistence of a belief in the generally different sexual and social mores of Singapore's European and "Asiatic" populations, the local colonial administration's long-held stance of the acceptability of noninterference in the intimate affairs of colonized communities gave way to an assured belief in the benefits of intervention.

The regulation of prostitution in the colony began in earnest in 1870 when legislation passed under the Contagious Diseases Ordinance set out requirements for the registration of brothels, the zoning of red light districts, and the medical examination of prostitutes.[15] These measures were intended to hamper the operation of unlicensed or "sly" brothels and to ensure the health of prostitutes in order to curb the spread of venereal diseases that, at the time, were increasingly crippling the colonial labor force. Over the next many decades, prostitution and its social consequences remained one of the most contentious issues faced by Singapore's governors. Frequent and heated debates featured constant tensions between in situ colonial authorities and representatives of the home colonial office along with metropolitan social reformers over the most appropriate way forward. While positions within these two groups were not uniform, external actors tended to push for abolition of the "social evil" while local officials favored regulation of what they saw in this colonial outpost with its peculiar social complex to be an evil, perhaps, but an undeniably necessary one.

In its 1923 report, the Venereal Diseases Committee, composed of local experts chosen by the Singapore colonial administration, states, "It is necessary . . . to emphasise the absolute and radical nature of the difference between life conditions in Singapore and those in any Western town; and to state in the most unanimous and emphatic manner the warning that any attempt to judge Singapore by Western methods is not only useless, but must be totally unjust, misleading and incorrect" (Straits Settlements 1923, 2–3). Furthermore, the committee makes the following recommendation: "After considering the evidence most carefully, and having due regard to the special conditions which govern life in the Straits Settlements, the Committee holds that, if the prostitutes are adequately looked after, a) Venereal Disease would be attacked at its fountain head; b) what is essential and practical could be attained; and c) the greatest of all blows would be struck at the prevalence of Syphilis and Gonorrhea" (Straits Settlements 1923, 8). A rather different view is put forward in the 1925 report of the Advisory Committee on Social Hygiene, a committee of external public health experts established by the British Colonial Office in London. This committee acknowledged that "the social conditions prevailing at Singapore are abnormal" since "the coolie class, uneducated and living in conditions of overcrowding," make up the majority population and a "marked disparity between the numbers of the sexes," especially among immigrant groups, prevails. But it disagreed emphatically with the Singapore colonial administration's response of brothel regulation coupled with periodic medical exams for prostitutes. Instead, finding prostitution morally repugnant for a range of reasons including its role in perpetuating the trafficking of young women and girls, this external committee argued for the closure of all brothels in the colony and the outright abolition of commercial sex work. Furthermore, it argued that if a skewed sex ratio led inevitably to the proliferation of prostitution, it was government's role to deal with the root cause: "We suggest that it should be the constant effort of the Administration to explore every avenue which would be likely to encourage female immigration, and especially to encourage the immigration of wives and children with their husbands."[16] In the view of this committee, population reform rather than population management was the better, and more ethical, long-term solution.

The colonial home office eventually enforced its position on prostitution, resulting in the closure of Singapore's "known" brothels in the late 1920s. The local administration continued to criticize the wisdom of this move for years to come. The following 1934 quote from Sir Roland Braddell, a leading barrister in colonial Singapore, summarizes the official position in the colony well: "The result has been sly prostitution and widespread venereal disease, ruined careers, and broken health, a terrible price to pay for moral enthusiasms. A dreadful mistake has been made" (Braddell 1934, quoted in Warren 2003, 176). Local and external colonial forces were not completely at odds, however. While no neat resolution to the issue of whether prostitution ought to be regulated or outlawed was arrived at, the two sides did agree on the need to alter Singapore's demographic composition. Indeed, such a view had been gaining steam among local colonial officials since around the turn of the twentieth century. The unbalanced sex ratio had by then of course long been on the minds of colonial officials. But from around 1900, references to this demographic fact noticeably multiply within the colonial administration's reports, studies, and correspondence with the home office. Furthermore, a nonneutral tone creeps into its representation. For instance, the colonial administration's annual report from 1900 notes with a tinge of anxiety that "the disproportion between the sexes still increases" (Straits Settlements 1900, 250), while the report from 1905 declares with some relief that "the steady increase in the proportion of women arriving is very satisfactory" (Straits Settlements 1905, 628). Such began the transition in the local colonial administration's stance toward the sex ratio that saw a generally noninterventionist position on matters of demographic composition give way to a profound commitment to population reform, a transition that was part of a broader shift in colonial policy away from a narrow emphasis on production alone and toward an approach that understood production as linked to social reproduction.

As Lenore Manderson states, "at the point that the British colonial government decided that the cost of continued immigration of laborers was greater than the cost of public health interventions within the colony, the child was discovered" (1997, 378). More bluntly put, in line with shifting ideas about the relationship between population and labor in Britain and other parts of its empire, "it seemed cheaper to nurture children to adulthood than to import adult workers" (Manderson 1996, 203). As the state became interested in reproduction in the early twentieth century, Manderson notes "a perceptible shift of policy and mood *from* that of protecting men *to* that of protecting women" as, alongside the maintenance of the local colonial administration's position that prostitution was a necessity in this male-dominated environment, it began to take modest initiatives aimed at combating high infant mortality rates and nurturing family life (1996, 191, emphasis original). For instance, the colonizers established clinics for maternal and child health, developed curricula for domestic science education, and created home visit programs for new mothers. Furthermore, in some circles, "the discourse of prostitution re-oriented to issues of morality and an alternative, contradictory model of sexuality that prescribed women's proper roles" (Manderson 1996, 192). Thus the proliferating references in colonial documents from the first two decades of the twentieth century to the abnormal sex ratio as a problem for Singapore's future growth and development coincide with the gradual extension of the colonial state's control over reproductive and domestic life. But while the colonial administration had begun to firmly desire a change in Singapore's demographics, it did not yet take very active steps toward fostering one. This would soon change.

In 1921, during discussions in the Legislative Council on the topic of venereal disease in the Straits Settlements, the medical officer, Dr. Galloway, stated, "Our call was for manhood in its full vigour and, as Nature has not yet provided a race of neuters for the hives of human activity, the consequences were a foregone conclusion. Prostitution is merely a matter of demand and supply and there is nothing abnormal in the prevalence of prostitution in these Colonies. It is the natural sequel to an abnormal social condition" (Straits Settlements 1921, B225). This line of thinking is obviously consonant with the overall view of the colonial administration that prostitution was a necessity in the colony given Singapore's particular demographic characteristics. But Dr. Galloway further stated, "*I fear I have been able to convey to you in a very imperfect manner a picture of the abnormal social complex which we have created for our economic needs and for which, and for the consequences of which, we must assume the responsibility*" (Straits Settlements 1921, B225, emphasis original). During the 1920s, the colonial administration began to "assume the responsibility" for the imbalanced sex ratio and its social consequences in earnest. Over the remainder of the colonial period, infant and maternal health was prioritized, a family planning association was founded, the Department of Social Welfare was established, the Chinese

Protectorate greatly increased its efforts to stem the trafficking of women and girls, and, most significantly, immigration policies were reconfigured to encourage family formation and reunification through the enactment of quotas on the entry of single male workers while migration remained open for women other than those entering for the purposes of prostitution. Through these initiatives and more, the colonial state dramatically expanded the extension of its reach into the reproductive and domestic lives of the colony's inhabitants that it had begun to undertake in the first two decades of the century. In other words, in these late colonial years, the British administration found the family as a tool for development.

Historian Loh Kah Seng argues that the many new bureaucratic mechanisms that were put in place during the late colonial period in order to foster family life "must be viewed as attempts to establish and extend the authority of the state" as the state "sought to lay the foundation for a modern, planned, sanitized and disciplined Singapore" (2007, 5).[17] Building on this point, I argue that this project to modernize, plan, sanitize, and discipline Singapore and its population through the extension of state authority over an intimate sphere must be understood simultaneously, and fundamentally, as a project of heteronormalization. In the first instance, this argument accounts for the fact that the family that the colonial governors sought to foster was most certainly a heterosexual one. More broadly, I argue thus because the shaping of the family as a primary unit of governance in late colonial Singapore involved not the idealization of simply heterosexual subjects but the idealization of very particular heterosexual subjects. A contest between "family values" and the "gay agenda" may dominate discussions over sexual citizenship in Singapore today. But though the late colonial government's interventions into the domestic lives of the colonized certainly created the conditions for an eventual contest between heterosexuality and homosexuality, this sexual binary did not animate them. Instead, late colonial population reform efforts honed in on weeding out what were deemed to be deviant heterosexualities among the colonized so that the proper family could take root.

A return to consideration of the local colonizers' views on prostitution sheds light on this point. Recall the Venereal Diseases Committee's emphasis on "the absolute and radical nature of the difference between life conditions in Singapore and those in any Western town." The imbalanced sex ratio was certainly seen by the colonizers as one important factor in shaping this radically different social situation. But they also held serious concerns over the "habits" of the colonized communities. The report of Venereal Diseases Committee hones in on "the attitude of the Chinese towards sex practice" in particular, stating,

> Among workmen and coolies and ricksha-pullers . . . experience has shown and the evidence tendered proves, that "morality" in the Western sense of the word,

simply does not exist. When opportunity and means are favourable, the Chinese sees no reason why he should not gratify his instincts. Moreover, it is an appalling fact—brought out all too clearly in the evidence—that among the middle class Chinese, consisting in the main of Hokkiens, Teochews, Cantonese and Hakkas, many of whom if not, indeed, most of whom are married, marital fidelity is almost entirely disregarded. The well-to-do Chinese patronises singing girls and frequents brothels heedless of the dangers which he may thence bring to his wife, or his wives and concubines. This is a curiously contradictory trait in the character of a race of otherwise good husbands and excellent fathers. (Straits Settlements 1923, 3)

Thus, while the local colonial administration agreed that balancing the sex ratio and facilitating family formation were in Singapore's best developmental interests, it held firm in its position that prostitution was a necessity in the colony long after the home colonial office insisted on the closure of brothels because it held particular views on the "nature" of the colonized population. It disagreed with the imposition of, as Sir Roland Braddell puts it in the quote above, "moral enthusiasms" from elsewhere in large part because it faced what it characterized as the "curious" cultural "traits" of the colonized.

As the largest colonized group, the various ethnic groups composing Singapore's Chinese community were the subjects of considerable scrutiny by the colonial administration. As noted above, it held that "the Asiatic regards prostitution and sex generally on a different plane to that of an European," and paid much attention to the purported proclivity toward prostitution among the Chinese community as a whole, and toward polygamy among that community's wealthier members. The local colonial administration regarded these proclivities as inherent and thus, as Philippa Levine states, its position that prostitution ought to be regulated rather than outlawed "looked 'back' to 'local' culture rather than 'forward' to modernity'" (1999, 38).[18] With the abolition of "known" brothels, the implementation of measures to balance the sex ratio, and the new emphasis on family formation of the late colonial period, however, the colonial administration began to concertedly push the colonized communities forward. In other words, the institution of a new heteronormative social frame in the late colonial period was at once a project of sexual propriety and one of racial uplift. Crucially, the colonial administration was not alone in this project. It found allies among elites within the colonized communities, most notably the Straits Chinese.[19]

The term "Straits Chinese" refers to persons of Chinese heritage who were born in the Straits Settlements. Many men from within this community of English-educated persons of a mercantile class were closely tied to the colonial administration as local informants. For instance, Straits Chinese men composed the Chinese Advisory Board that directly reported to the colonial office of the Chinese Protectorate, and their most well respected members sat on the Legisla-

tive Council as "unofficials" (i.e., nominated members of the colonized community who acted as consultants for the colonial administration). Their efforts to fit
into the project of colonial modernity were duly rewarded with the admiration
of the colonial administration. The following declaration of this admiration,
made by C. W. Darbishire on the event of the retirement of Tan Jiak Kim from
his "unofficial" position on the Legislative Council, demonstrates its depth:

> The Chinese community bulks very largely in the life of these Settlements, and we
> who are in daily touch with the Chinese cannot fail to realize how overwhelmingly
> the welfare of these Settlements depends upon their goodwill and upon a mutual
> understanding. This goodwill, this understanding, this confidence in British rule
> which we have here is unhesitatingly granted to us, and we recognize that it is so
> granted to us in no small degree because we have been fortunate in finding men
> ready to assist us amongst *the enlightened members of the Chinese. These leaders are
> broad-minded enough to grasp the Western point of view and to weld it easily and
> smoothly with the Eastern point of view.* (Straits Settlements 1915, B30, emphasis
> added)

As this quote suggests, the Straits Chinese and other colonized elites occupied
an ambivalent position within the colonial hierarchy. At once "a liberal subject
and an object of colonial difference," this group pushed back against many colonial policies at the same time that they were also rendered complicit in the
construction of representations of backward colonized others and advocated
societal reforms intended to "civilize" the rest of the colonized community (Goh
2010, 483). As Yao Souchou argues, "The loyal British Chinese, socially respectable and tradition-bound, could come into being only by their silent referencing
to the Other Chinese mired in the world of opium, prostitutes and criminal
violence. For the Straits Chinese, the mass of their countrymen must be transformed by modern education and health measures . . . in order to achieve their
new destiny as loyal British Chinese" (Yao 1999, 117).

Since the end of the nineteenth century, certain prominent Straits Chinese
men undertook what Philip Holden has referred to as a "body project," or "a
disciplinary regime of self-care, in order to re-create themselves as modern subjects" (Holden 1999, 59). Specifically, they aimed to counter what they saw as
a spirit of hedonism that had led to the degeneration of their community. In
their discourse, "physical and moral continence were repeatedly stressed" as
they "juxtapos[ed] appeals against public spitting with exhortations to monogamy" (Holden 1999, 66–67). Like the colonial administration, since around
the turn of the century, they too depicted the imbalanced sex ratio as a problem in need of redress. In 1921, Song Ong Siang, speaking as an "unofficial" in
the Legislative Council on the "reduction of the disparity between the sexes,"
stated,

This is a remarkable advance when we look back to, say, 50 years ago when the proportion was something like 1 to 12. This fact is very encouraging in the interests of the moral welfare of the Chinese people—the largest community of the population. A steady influx of Chinese women as wives and intended spouses of the Chinese traders and workmen in the Colony should be encouraged, as, in a large measure, this should become an effective antidote to, and counteract the evils of, hetairism [concubinage]. (Straits Settlements 1921, B223)

Also like the colonial administration, the Straits Chinese elites decried improper family lives as an impediment to Singapore's progress and development. Song Ong Siang again, this time writing in the *Straits Chinese Magazine* in 1897, states, "Are we not desirous that the Straits-born Chinese community shall be looked upon as an educated and enlightened people? Then let us look after our women, and help them all we can to be themselves more enlightened, more perfect, more noble in their thoughts and aspirations, and more fit to be the worthy mothers of the future citizens of this Settlement" (Song 1897, 17). Thus the colonial administration's late colonial modernizing push was underpinned in large part by interventions into the intimate lives of the colony's inhabitants and incorporated efforts to recast expectations and perceptions of a migrant community along the lines of gender, race, and class. It was, furthermore, by no means merely a British imposition given the widespread popularity of reformist sentiments among the colonized elites.[20] Certain members of the colonized communities undertook a project of modernization in concert with colonial officials and, as the next subsections show through discussion of the cases of marriage policy and housing reform, the colonizer-colonized relationship consequentially shaped the direction in which the Singapore family was taken.

Marrying into Modernity

Ann Stoler, in her work on the Dutch East Indies, exposes intimacy as a central facet of colonial governance. She highlights the ways in which the bodies of colonizers were "never in fact isolated, but defined by intimate relationships and daily contacts of a special kind" (Stoler 1995, 111). A racialized, gendered, and sexualized bourgeois project, she argues, was thus made in the colonies rather than imported to them. The idea of Europeanness was maintained through the negotiation of boundaries between white administrators (and particularly their wives) and their native servants and nursemaids. Also among the "tensions of empire" that she carefully details are anxieties over mixed marriages and the fate of mixed-race children.[21] Indeed, as Tamara Loos notes, "Colonial regimes most rigorously controlled marriages that involved elites and 'Europeans' because . . . these marriages helped regulate who belonged to the ruling class" (2008, 31). But they much less rigorously controlled unions that did not involve at least one European. In these cases, which constituted the vast majority, the state deferred to the colonized themselves. In the Straits Settlements, marriage within the Indian community was to be administered according to the principles of Hinduism, "Mahomedan" law guided Malay marriage, and Chinese marriage was left to Chinese custom. This neat description is deceptive, however, for the principle of noninterference worked on a more theoretical than literal level as the colonial government had much to say about the marriage customs of those it ruled, not least because it regarded its own monogamous form of marriage to be the pinnacle of civility. The legislation of Chinese marriage is exemplary of this fact.

In 1930, an appellate court judge in Penang (another corner of the Straits Settlements) ruled in a case that was brought to determine the legitimacy of a son's claims by a woman other than the wife of his Chinese father's estate. In doing so, he remarked, "the modifications of the law of England which obtain in the Colony in the application of that law to the various alien races established there, arise from the necessity of preventing the injustice or oppression which would ensure if that law were applied to alien races unmodified."[22] After the statement of this lofty ambition, he went on to assert that "from the above-mentioned necessity arises the recognition by the Courts of the Colony of polygamous marriages among the Chinese."[23] This latter statement is common to numerous judgments of colonial courts on matters pertaining to the inheritances of wealthy Chinese men. It had been taken as legal fact that the Chinese were polygamous since the ruling in the precedent-setting "Six Widows" case of 1908. But this claim was far from unchallenged within the Chinese community, particularly by members of the Straits Chinese elite. Many of the most prominent members of this group made very public their disapproval of the nonrequirement of registration of Chinese marriages and the colonial determination that such marriages were customarily polygamous. After years in which successive "unofficials" raised the issue of Chinese marriage in the Legislative Council, the colonial administration formed a Chinese Marriage Committee to report on the issue in 1926. The only European member of the committee was its chair, the acting secretary for Chinese affairs, while the remaining members were drawn from the Straits Chinese community. The committee's work was led by two unofficials, Song Ong Siang and Tan Cheng Lock, and its terms of reference were as follows: "To report on the customs, rites and ceremonies, observed by the Chinese resident in the Straits Settlements and to submit, if thought desirable, proposals for legislation as to what forms or ceremonies should constitute a valid marriage and as to the registration of such marriages" (*Report of the Chinese Marriage Committee* 1926, 1). It approached this task by soliciting the views of Chinese associations, clan groups, and members of the public.

When the work of the committee was done, it reported that opposition to the registration of Chinese marriages was far more widespread than was support.

Cited reasons for this stance were "the dislike of government interference with marriage which has long been managed by the people themselves" and "fear that registration would be used to enforce monogamy in the future" (*Report of the Chinese Marriage Committee* 1926, 4). Furthermore, the point is centrally made that opinion was divided between the numerical minority of those born in the colony and the numerical majority of those born in China. The report states, "The District Associations and other societies whose members are composed entirely or in part of Chinese born in China, are almost entirely opposed to registration of Chinese marriages in any shape or form; and this opposition was voiced in most cases by the China-born witnesses" (*Report of the Chinese Marriage Committee* 1926, 5). But by casting the locally born as "more advanced" members of the community, the committee's report recommends registration on a voluntary basis. Its justification for this recommendation is spelled out as follows: "We consider that probably in the first instance only Chinese born in the colony or Malaya would make use of the provision, but that as its advantages are recognized, it will become increasingly used" (*Report of the Chinese Marriage Committee* 1926, 7). In discussions of the report in the Legislative Council, Song Ong Siang tried to push this recommendation through by insisting, "There is no doubt that the trend of opinion among the educated, intelligent and advanced sections of the Chinese community of this Colony,—both men and women,—is in favour of legislation, in some form, for registration of Chinese marriages,—of a voluntary character to begin with, if compulsory registration should be decried by the Chinese community as objectionable" (Straits Settlements 1927, B27).

The Legislative Council chose not to go forward with the registration of Chinese marriages in any form on the basis that the report had found little desire for it. Yet the Straits Chinese unofficials continued to raise the issue in the Council. The clearest assertion of the motivation behind this continued drive is found in the impassioned speech of Lim Cheng Ean in 1933:

> I have brought up this question because as a father of growing daughters I feel that I must be able to marry off my daughters in the same way as you Europeans marry yours—give them the new freedom and not let them be tied up and at the mercy of brutes. . . . You now exclude the Chinese from China by the Aliens Ordinance, because you want to build a new nationality, a new nation of Straits Settlements people. Give us this then. If other people don't want it, let them not come into it. (Straits Settlements 1933, B107)

He would have to wait until the 1961 passage of the Women's Charter by the People's Action Party government—a development discussed in the next chapter—to see this vision of governmental regulation of marriage become reality. With this legislation, polygamy was outlawed and registration of all marriages became a legal requirement. Only then was the law of the former colony that Tan Cheng Lock had described as "a half-caste offspring resulting from the mating of English law to Chinese law by our Judges" finally made Singaporean (Straits Settlements 1933, B101).

Housing the "Normal Family"

I turn now to housing policy, an arena in which Singapore is today seen as a global leader thanks to its extensive postcolonial public housing program. Very shortly after its inception in 1960, the Housing and Development Board had, in its own words, "broken the backbone of Singapore's acute and, at one time, seemingly insoluble Housing problem."[24] By 1965, it had already built fifty-four thousand units, well more than doubling the twenty-three thousand that the colonial administration's Singapore Improvement Trust (SIT) had constructed over its twenty-three-year history. Given this impressive early expansion of the public housing program and its consolidation over subsequent decades, SIT has long been deemed a failure and HDB a success. As such, HDB tends to be understood as a phenomenon of Singapore's postcolonial era.[25] But as Loh points out, "the ideological distance between the British colonial regime and the PAP is not as great as portrayed in most scholarship" (Loh 2007, 2). Thus despite the considerable differences in scale of SIT and HDB activities, the specific continuities and discontinuities between these colonial and postcolonial housing initiatives are worth exploring. For though the postcolonial housing program numerically eclipses its predecessor's accomplishments, definition of the type of households that HDB houses reaches consequentially back into the colonial period. Indeed, housing interventions have been a significant mode of social control in Singapore since the colonial government began to remark upon "insanitary conditions" as a serious social problem, along with the problem of population, around the turn of the twentieth century. At that time, overcrowded housing arrangements were highlighted as a fundamental concern and two major housing studies were commissioned that resulted in the publication of the *Report on the Sanitary Conditions of Singapore* (Simpson 1907) and *Proceedings and Report of the Commission Appointed to Inquire into the Cause of the Present Housing Difficulties in Singapore and the Steps Which Should Be Taken to Remedy Such Difficulties* (Singapore 1918). Both set out what their authors depict as major shortcomings in housing conditions. These include inadequate space between buildings, improper drainage, lack of light and air, and the absence of back-lanes. Ameliorating these conditions would be a main preoccupation of colonial administrators interested in social welfare throughout the remainder of the colonial period.

In a landmark study on colonial Singapore as contested urban space, Brenda Yeoh (1996) meticulously details the great lengths to which British administrators went to impose "scientific principles" of urban planning from the western world. She considers the ways in which a variety of urban planning initiatives, among them many housing proposals and programs, aimed to reshape the values and behavior of colonized communities. Evidence of racism and cultural bias is indeed abundant in the 1907 and 1918 housing reports. For instance, the acting municipal health officer states, "The Asiatic does not like air in his dwelling-house. It does not matter how many windows or ventilation openings there are, he always endeavours to close them up, so that custom does away with any good that well-designed houses are intended to produce" (Singapore 1918, C17). In another example, the editor of the English-language daily newspaper the *Straits Times* states,

> The lowest classes in the West have nothing to learn from the East in the matter of crass carelessness and filthiness, but there is one noteworthy difference. In the West, extreme filth is almost invariably associated with extreme poverty, and that poverty can almost invariably be traced to vice and intemperance. But in the East one finds huge numbers of people who are sober, law-abiding, and moderately prosperous living under conditions which similar classes in the West would not tolerate. (Singapore 1918, C102)

Furthermore, the report lists "habits, customs and tastes of Asiatics" that are purported to adversely affect health such as "careless[ness] in the disposal of refuse and nightsoil," "preparation of food under insanitary conditions," "use of polluted wells and the universal habit of spitting" (Singapore 1918, C81).

Despite this overall reformist tone, however, the 1907 and 1918 housing reports that sought to identify housing problems and their potential solutions did not problematize the composition of households or suggest that it ought to be altered. Overcrowding was seen to have two components: the "overcrowding of areas with houses" and the "overcrowding of houses with inhabitants" (Simpson 1907, 29). Much emphasis was placed on the latter, and detailed studies of the carving up of individual dwellings into numerous cubicles that sheltered groups of bachelors, single families plus lodgers, multiple families, or other configurations were carried out. Many suggestions were given to improve the state of the cubicles—for example, more lighting and better sanitation—but cubicle living itself was not critiqued. Rather, it was seen as an inevitable and necessary mode of dwelling. In the 1907 report, this view is clearly stated as follows: "It is a Sisyphus task to attempt to do away with cubicles. It is well to recognize the fact that cubicles are a necessity considering the nature of the population of Singapore" (Simpson 1907, A64). So while the sanitary practices of "Asiatics" were seen as amenable to reform, the facts of the population itself were not. That is, the demographic characteristics of an unsettled, migrant-majority population and a highly unbalanced sex ratio were not identified as social problems in need of redress, a position that was in line with dominant colonial administration views on population issues at the time.[26] One commentator even went so far as to suggest that the colonized population had adapted so well to the situation in Singapore that it was now part of their culture to live in close quarters. In the acting municipal health officer's words, "Man is a gregarious animal, and this attribute is very much emphasized among Asiatics, especially amongst the working class. As far as I can make out, they prefer to huddle together. . . . The crowding together has become a habit or custom" (Singapore 1918, C16–17).

As discussed above, by the 1920s the inordinately migrant and male population did however come to be seen as an obstacle to development by the colonial administration, and while the administration began to put in place immigration controls to limit the entry of single male workers while maintaining open migration for women other than prostitutes, it also established SIT in 1927 to address housing issues. Throughout the rest of the colonial period, this government agency worked toward providing dwellings suitable for migrant workers as well as families. On the latter front, SIT was not out of step with the Straits Settlements courts discussed above as it was also concerned with housing those "considered as forming a 'family unit' having regard to the family customs of the community."[27] It must be noted that SIT officials did not make determinations of customary families easily. As noted by an estates manager in 1947, "to attempt to define 'family customs' is extremely difficult." But SIT "were of the opinion that if two families desire to be rehoused together, they were bona fide relatives and so long as the 'custom family' consists of five persons it could be accepted."[28] The trust's "Housing Visitors" were advised to consider the following as "authorized" occupiers: "(a) Immediate members of the tenant's family, i.e. sons and daughters, married or unmarried and living with the family at all times. (b) Grandparents. (c) Aunts and uncles. (d) Cousins, including nieces and nephews. (e) Blood brother and blood sisters unmarried. (f) Legally adopted sons and daughters. (g) Widow or widower, i.e. sons or daughters married who have lost their wives or husbands and including their children if unmarried."[29] In delimiting bureaucratic guidelines, therefore, SIT did manipulate the notion of acceptable forms of kinship in the colony. But it nonetheless maintained a concern with the "family customs" of the colonized.

The Housing Development Board (HDB), formed in 1960 during Singapore's transitional period between colonial and postcolonial governance, took a different approach, however. Then, and to the present day, to purchase an HDB flat, the applicant must be twenty-one years of age and "form a proper family nucleus," which is defined as the applicant and fiancé(e); the applicant, spouse, and children (if any); the applicant, the applicant's parents, and siblings (if any); if widowed/divorced, the applicant and children under the applicant's legal custody; and, if orphaned, the applicant and unmarried siblings.[30] The meaning of and impetus for this change in focus can be gleaned from various studies on social and housing conditions that were conducted throughout the late 1940s and 1950s. They were carried out at the behest of the colonial government by both colonial officials and selected members of the colonized elite. As Loh has argued, these studies can be seen "as a type of 'reform literature' seeking to establish official control over indigenous forms of housing by representing them as areas of social pollution" (2007, 7). They are part of the reformist attitude that was well entrenched toward the end of colonial rule. The attitude of the administration is summed up in the Department of Social Welfare's 1950 Annual Report: "It must be admitted that the social welfare problems of Singapore are themselves well-nigh insuperable and that they are certainly incapable of solution unless there comes about, or is brought about, a deeper sense of responsibility in the average citizen of Singapore combined perhaps with a radical change in the social habits of a large part of the population" (Department of Social Welfare 1950).

Two of the most significant publications on social issues in Singapore published during the late colonial period were *A Social Survey of Singapore* (Department of Social Welfare 1947) and *Urban Incomes and Housing* (Goh 1956). Both studies were conducted by the Department of Social Welfare under the supervision of Goh Keng Swee. Born in Malacca, and thus a member of the Straits Chinese community, Goh completed his undergraduate and graduate degrees in economics at the London School of Economics and University of London before returning to the Straits Settlements as director of the Singapore Department of Social Welfare's Social and Economic Research Division. He eventually resigned this position to join the People's Action Party and became minister of finance in the first post-independence government under Prime Minister Lee Kuan Yew. Goh "was quick to pick up on trends sweeping Western social science, modernization theory most notably," and his fondness for Weberian thought heavily influenced his approach to government (Doshi and Coclanis 1999, 36). Indeed, "unlike many economists of his generation, who were focusing more on readily quantifiable variables, Goh always recognized the importance of culture and institutions in the process of economic development" (Doshi and Coclanis 1999, 36).

The institution of the family was central to Goh's thinking about Singapore's socioeconomic development. In *A Social Survey of Singapore*, he finds the fact that "house" and "household" were not identical in colonial Singapore society to be a significant impediment to progress: "The normal notion of a house as a place exclusive to the household dwelling therein has little relevance to the facts of the situation in Singapore and points to the absence of typical household sizes and the large percentage of single person households as particularly problematic (Department of Social Welfare 1947, 67). The report offers UK family composition patterns for comparison and on this basis determines that only those households that "have as their heads married men . . . may therefore be taken to represent the number of households which are organized on a normal family basis" (1947, 37). In the *Urban Incomes and Housing* report, Goh more specifically characterizes the normal family as "a kinship group of man, wife and children" and again emphasizes the abnormality of Singapore society due to the lack of coincidence between "family" and "household" (Goh 1956, 28). In this and other studies, household types are quantified "to separate the biological family type of household grouping—man, wife and children—from the others" with, notably, the normal and abnormal distinctions being attributed to settled and immigrant communities respectively (Goh 1956, 39).[31] As Goh notes, "Recent trends in Chinese immigration have of course helped both to 'normalize' the sex ratio of the population as well as to reduce the numbers of the unattached adult male immigrant. In recent years this latter result is achieved directly by the granting of entry permits to wives in China of persons resident in Singapore. . . . Despite all these developments there are still sizeable numbers of immigrants, both male and female, who do not lead normal family lives" (1956, 41). Thus, "family customs" and the "nature of the population" were both firmly on the agenda as the colonial administration began in earnest to cede responsibility for Singapore's development to the colonized elite.

The concern with creating "normal" families would stay with Goh throughout his days as a key figure in Singapore's post-independence government. For instance, in 1972, he argued, "In many poor countries, kinship ties impose certain economic obligations that are absent in Western countries where welfare and social security schemes assist those whose sources of incomes have been disrupted through old age, illness or unemployment. The extended or joint family system, by placing these functions on the income earners of the extended family, diminishes their capacity to save and may even reduce incentives to earn more income" (Goh 1972, 63). During his time as a prominent PAP minister, he emerged as a strong critic of what he referred to as "backward" peasant societies and "antiquated social customs and institutions." As the subsequent chapter shows, the imprint of these ideas can be seen in the modern family ideal that is still championed in contemporary Singapore.

Governing Intimacy

In this chapter, I have taken PM Lee's cue, in his 2007 speech to Parliament on his government's decision to uphold Section 377A of Singapore's Penal Code, that the preservation of the family is what is fundamentally at stake in debates over sexual norms in the city-state. I have also taken his guidance in framing a response to this fact, picking up on his point that the particular family norm— and thus the particular heteronormative logic—upon which Singapore's government officials claim that the city-state's development rests is the product of much work. Having traced the emergence of the "Singapore family" in the archival record, I argue that a colonial-era anti-sodomy law is still on the books in postcolonial Singapore not because it is a colonial throwback that has no place in contemporary Singapore society, and not because the city-state is just not postcolonial enough, but because the establishment of heteronormativity was a key facet of the transition from colonial administration to postcolonial governance. While the debates in Singapore over the persistence of Penal Code Section 377A have drawn a line between heterosexuality and homosexuality, following PM Lee's suggestion that this binary is central to the colonial-postcolonial relationship uncovers a much more complex intimate sphere than the sexual binary can capture. Thus the benefit of a postcolonial queer approach that takes the legacy of colonialism seriously and seeks to understand the links between sex, intimacy, citizenship, governance, and modernity.

Singapore's late colonial archival record contains few details on official perceptions of the threat that homosexuality was deemed to pose to the colonial project. But it bursts with explicit evidence of a bureaucratic project that made strong associations between modern aspirations and the need to recast race, gender, class, *and* sexual relation to form a proper domestic sphere. Any histories of sexuality in Singapore must therefore go beyond emphasis on the politics of homosexuality versus heterosexuality to explore what Foucault (1978) calls a sexual truth regime. Penal Code Section 377A stands because a specific mode of heteronormativity that was constructed in place during Singapore's late colonial period became an active and influential force in its development as an independent city-state. The establishment of intimate norms in both past and present has produced convictions regarding the appropriateness of sexual object choices to be sure. But it has also rendered family, kinship, and domesticity as central areas of governmental intervention in contemporary Singapore across multiple modes of identification. As a result, as the next chapter shows, to fulfill desires for modernity, development, and progress, not just LGBT people have been "queered" in the postcolonial city-state—so have the single, the uneducated, the "unskilled" migrant worker, and many others who have been deemed incapable of creating and sustaining a "quality" population within the logic of reproductive futurism that guides Singapore's development.

CHAPTER 4

Making the Modern Model Family at Home

> The family is the basic building block of our society. It has been so and, by policy,
> we have reinforced this and we want to keep it so. And by "family" in Singapore, we
> mean one man one woman, marrying, having children and bringing up children within
> that framework of a stable family unit.
> —PM Lee Hsien Loong (2007)

> In Singapore, the nuclear family consisting of husband, wife and unmarried children
> has long been the predominant family type since the 1950s.
> —Aline K. Wong and Stephen H. K. Yeh (1985)

The 1957 Singapore census report states that census takers were instructed to
define a household as

> a unit comprising a number of persons living together and having common food ar-
> rangements. By "common food arrangements" was meant the sharing in one or more
> of the processes of buying, cooking, serving and eating of food. It followed therefore
> that a household could consist of one person having his own separate food arrange-
> ments, whether or not he lived with others, or any number of persons irrespective of
> inter-relationship provided they lived together and had common food arrangements.
> It also followed that boarders, visitors, non-paying guests, resident servants and em-
> ployees and their families who were provided with food, were included as part of a
> household. On the other hand, lodgers, resident servants and employees and their
> families who were not provided with food, were treated as separate households. A
> group of residents of a mess where food arrangements were on a common basis, or
> a group of "amahs" living in an "amah kongsi" where there was a system of common
> food arrangements was treated as a household. (Department of Statistics 1957)

This task was obviously a complicated one, as it had likewise been for those col-
lecting data for prior British Malaya censuses.[1] By contrast, the 1970 census report
states,

> The identification and numbering of households in the census was . . . a relatively easy exercise especially as the majority of households consisted of family nucleus units which were easily identifiable and generally satisfied the twin conditions of "living together and sharing common food arrangements." Problems relating to the inclusion of persons with the household or the creation of separate households were limited to non-family nucleus units and in the case of family members to those who were not regularly living with the households. (Department of Statistics 1970, 18)

Of course, the key difference in context between these two reports is that independence was achieved between their printings. The 1970 document acknowledges this fact, stating, "Government's vigorous implementation of development programmes relating to industrialization and economic expansion, housing, education, family planning and other socio-economic fields since it took over power in 1959 has resulted in fundamental changes in the basic demographic and economic framework of the population" (Department of Statistics 1970, 1–2).

Upon reading the 1970 census report, one can almost hear the sigh of relief. After all, as the previous chapter demonstrates, when Singapore was a colonial entrepôt composed largely of single, male migrant workers, its "abnormal" population was a local concern from at least the early 1900s. By 1970, the postcolonial government had changed the composition of Singapore society, in good measure through efforts to "upgrade" the family. It had moved ahead with the late colonial efforts to create a proper domestic sphere with tremendous zeal, fulfilling "the project of governmentality of which colonialism dreamed, but which it could never realize" (Holden 2003, 313) and becoming "the best-known example in a market economy of a state restructuring society" (Salaff 2004, 261).

Thus, when PM Lee Hsien Loong asserted in 2007 that the family is a "basic building block" of Singapore society, he was speaking in commonsense terms, with the force of decades upon decades of work behind him. As a result of this work, the family has been cemented as one of Singapore's Shared Values, a pillar on which its socioeconomic foundation is built.[2] As Vivian Balakrishnan, then minister for community development, youth, and sports, put it in 2009,

> The Family remains as an anchor for individuals and the cornerstone of society. Strong and stable families are crucial to our wellbeing. They serve as the first line of care and support for an individual, and lay the foundation for the building of communities, and eventually, the nation. The Family is the only institution that creates and nurtures the next generation. It is therefore the cradle of our future. (Singapore National Family Council and Ministry of Community Development, Youth and Sports 2009)

Such grandiose narrative treatments of family are abundant in Singapore's everyday state discourse. Through government speeches, educational curricula, media outputs, social programs, and more, public life is liberally peppered with pronouncements on the family as fundamental to socioeconomic development.

Given the centrality of the family to Singapore society, economy, and politics, a substantial body of scholarly literature weighs in on the PAP's contemporary population policies. Much of it, particularly that which is policy oriented and produced in conjunction with, or within arm's length of, government agencies, is in step with the PAP's aims and guides it in its efforts. Then there is the more critical literature, which is a much smaller body of work. In it, as I show below, critics point out the contradictory logics that underpin the Singapore family and offer ways forward that overcome these tensions. The critical literature highlights that the PAP's anti-welfarist, race-based, and gender-biased policies create a climate in which it is difficult for many Singapore families to thrive. In this chapter, I build on these important points to extend this book's queer reading of Singapore's developmental logic and to extend the critical literature on the Singapore family. I also look at the ways in which family policy in Singapore is closely tied to the other key policy areas of housing and migration, and thus touch on and add to debates in those fields.

To queer the Singapore family, it must be noted that this is an institution that is currently articulated and structured through discourse and policy in ways that work deliberately and completely to police the homosexual-heterosexual binary. The Singapore family is a nuclear one, built around an opposite-sex cisgender couple, full stop. Surprisingly, this point is very rarely made, and only ever in passing, in the existing critical Singapore studies literature on family, housing, and migration. It is a point made more forcefully within the queer and sexuality studies literature on the city-state, though, as mentioned in chapter 1. So this fact is on the radar within the broader field of Singapore studies. But to queer the Singapore family in the more capacious sense that animates this book's analysis requires going further than identifying it as heterosexist. It requires identifying it as heteronormative and as thus sustained by sexual logics as well as and inextricably from logics around race, class, gender, and nationality. Then, upon making these connections plain, it requires moving away from focusing on how the Singapore state might better shore up this norm to instead question whether, as currently conceptualized, it is a norm that ought to be shored up.

In this chapter, I first provide a brief historical account of the ways that the PAP government intensely picked up the late colonial interest in fostering the family form as part of its efforts to spur on Singapore's takeoff for modernization, and then carried this concern forward through its family and housing policies, which remain generally consistent to the present day, even though age of first marriage has long been rising while fertility levels have long been falling. Then I survey some existing critical scholarship on the family in Singapore that shows that it is a meritocratic-eugenic institution that, yes, offers some comfort and support, but also fosters exclusion, precarity, and disenfranchisement.

Finally, I further this point by shifting the focus away from concern with how the city-state's demographic "problems" might be overcome in order to take the state's "failure" seriously as evidence of the instability of the unit at the center of hegemonic notions of appropriate intimacy, and as an opportunity to robustly challenge the developmental narrative that the city-state's family norm supports. While critical literature on the Singapore family generally focuses on the way in which this norm has been put in place through family planning and housing policies, by looking at the ways in which the colonial concern with "abnormal population" has resurfaced in its contemporary migration policies I argue that the Singapore family needs not just reform but serious rethinking.

From Quantity to "Quality"

As discussed at length in chapter 3, the colonial administration expanded its interest in production to encompass social reproduction in the last decades of its rule, taking extensive measures since the 1920s to balance the sex ratio and foster family life. By 1955, just two years before the British agreed to self-rule and the PAP assumed office, the administration was already seeing the sort of transformation it had been working toward. For instance, the *Master Plan* of 1955 states: "A former characteristic of the population was the predominance of males, which largely conditioned the type of community activity. . . . Since the war, numerically sex equality has become more marked, and a new pattern of social contact has emerged" (Singapore 1955a, 29). So the stage was set. As Wong and Yeh (1985) note in the second epigraph above, the nuclear family had become the predominant family type, and the PAP could invest in its modernization.

Crucially, in undertaking its reform efforts, the new government put much more explicit emphasis on reworking the "customs" of the population than the colonial administration had. In particular, it stressed the need to instill new norms and a strong sense of social responsibility, in good measure by casting Singapore society as meritocratic. As Goh Keng Swee wrote in 1966, "I believe that unless democratic countries can create new institutions and promote new values which can galvanize, inspire, cajole, induce and, in the last resort, compel men into action, they will not be able to lift themselves out of the present state of stagnation and poverty" (quoted in Kwok 1999, 50). Or, consider then prime minister Lee Kuan Yew's 1969 statement that the government needed to put policies in place "so that the irresponsible, the social delinquents do not believe that all they have to do is to produce their children and the government then owes them and their children sufficient food, medicine, housing, education, and jobs" (quoted in Salaff 1988, 37).

As stated above, the family was a key domain on which the postcolonial PAP trained its efforts to discipline Singapore's population. In the realm of family law, as Eddie Kuo and Aline Wong put it, "Once the P.A.P. came into power, one of its first tasks was to bring order and uniformity into the prevailing legal chaos" (1979, 8). The Women's Charter became law in 1961, with the primary aims of outlawing polygamy for all non-Muslims and requiring registration of all marriages. In September 1965, immediately on the heels of Singapore's expulsion from Malaysia, the *White Paper on Family Planning* was presented to the newly independent city-state's Parliament. This document, like many other government and civil society documents in 1960s Singapore, clearly links developmental aims with family limitation: "If we look at Singapore society itself or any sophisticated society for that matter, it is clear that the more well-to-do and better educated strata of society generally have small families of 2 or at most 3 children." It claims that the government ought to aim, through family planning policies, to "liberate our women from the burden of bearing and raising an unnecessarily large number of children" and to thus "increase human happiness for all." In sum, the white paper states, "By restricting the number of babies born each year, there will not only be increased happiness for mothers but also for their families and we can at the same time, improve the general welfare of our people by raising living standards, through channelising millions more of public funds into productive economic development of Singapore and thus to increase more job opportunities and prosperity, all round" (Singapore 1965). This advice was taken up wholeheartedly. As Yong Nyuk Lin, the first post-independence minister for health, stated, "Family Planning is . . . a matter of national importance and indeed, one of urgency for us. Our best chances for survival in an independent Singapore is stress on quality and not on quantity" (Singapore Family Planning and Population Board 1968).

With such pronouncements, the work of building a distinctly Singaporean family began in earnest. Whereas the colonial administration's Family Planning Association, founded in 1949, was a strictly voluntary organization, the PAP formed a new Singapore Family Planning and Population Board (FPPB) in 1966. For the next eighteen years, FPPB sought to foster a "quality" population through antinatalist policies. For instance, voluntary sterilization was legalized in 1969, and between 1969 and 1988, 112,568 sterilizations were performed; induced abortion was also legalized in 1969, and between 1969 and 1988, 288,666 abortions were performed; and a range of tax disincentives for higher order births were rolled out in 1973 (Drakakis-Smith et al. 1993). These policies were bolstered by the fact that the Singapore family norm that the PAP sought to achieve was very literally put into place in the city-state's flats.[3] Nation-building objectives and housing goals have been closely intertwined in Singapore throughout its postcolonial period. The Housing Development Board (HDB), which was formed by the People's Action Party (PAP) government in 1960 to provide "homes for the people," has since then progressively covered the island with modernist high-rise apartment blocks in which more than 85 percent of the current population resides. Thus the two meanings of "domestic," as both residential dwelling and national territory, collide unusually forcefully in this context, and national family policy has been closely tied to the city-state's housing policy since HDB's inception. Recall its tenancy requirements, which were established in 1960 and remain unchanged today. To purchase an HDB flat, the applicant must be twenty-one years of age and "form a proper family nucleus," which is defined as the applicant and fiancé(e); the applicant, spouse, and children (if any); the applicant, the applicant's parents, and siblings (if any); if widowed/divorced, the applicant, and children under the applicant's legal custody; and, if orphaned, the applicant and unmarried siblings.[4]

To point to the ways in which the organization has sought to shape Singapore's familial subjects into "quality" citizens, I turn here to its in-house magazine *Our Home* as an expression of the sort of lives HDB sought to foster within its flats.[5] This free publication was distributed to all HDB tenants between 1972 and 1989, and as Jane Jacobs and Stephen Cairns observe, it perpetuated "ideas about . . . how one can be modern, or, even, how one can be Singaporean" (2008, 573).[6] It encouraged readers to become courteous and responsible residents who make the most of life in their modern flats and covered much ground in this regard. Some of the recurring topics include nutrition, food preparation and menu planning, interior design and decorating tips, instructions for the use of modern household appliances, advice on how to deal with elevator malfunctions, and procedures for refuse disposal. Across this range of topics and more, the intended target audience remains the family. No matter what the advice, it is for husbands and wives, or alternatively breadwinners and homemakers, tasked with the responsibility of building and reproducing the young nation.

That the publication's overarching goal is to build happy, productive families comes across most strikingly in its covers over the years. Across seventy-two issues, thirty covers present unpopulated images of various HDB building projects. The remainder are focused on HDB inhabitants and, more specifically, its families. In thirty-nine of these forty-two covers, *Our Home*'s tenant readership is presented with images of parents and/or grandparents with children, children alone, and, in a few instances, three generations together. Inhabitants are shown sometimes in portrait style close-up but far more often as active participants in the HDB experience. They are shown sharing meals either in their flats or at neighborhood food centers, enjoying amenities such as playgrounds, sports fields, and public pools, and participating in cultural festivals and holiday celebrations.

Of course, as already stated, HDB made tenancy available only to those who conformed to its definition of a "proper family nucleus" from its inception. Thus the tendency to represent this group on its magazine's cover, rather than acknowledging the diversity of household forms that still had a strong presence in wider Singapore society well into the 1970s, is unsurprising. Flipping past the cover and delving into its pages, however, the degree to which HDB was involved not merely in housing this specific family form but in shaping it becomes apparent. The existence of strong links between HDB and FPPB are evident in a consistent concern with family size in the articles. For example, under the title "Happy Families," residents are informed that "the love and care in a large family of six to ten children must necessarily be of a different kind and quality. Out of sheer necessity, parents are likely to run their homes autocratically, stressing more on the simple mechanics of outward conformity than on the inner dynamics of children."[7] "The guidance clinic" discusses a child exhibiting symptoms of withdrawal and states that he, "like many other cases, came from a large family. He lived in HDB one-room flat with his parents and five brothers and sisters. His father did not have a regular income."[8] Along similar lines, young couples are informed that early marriage and childbearing will lead to "agonizing marital problems," "shorter birth intervals and large completed family size," and pregnancies "prone to complications" and "higher incidence of prematurity and low birthweight."[9]

Most explicitly, space in the magazine is generously allotted for FPPB advertisements containing slogans such as "girl or boy, two is enough" and "small families brighter future" as well as article contributions by the board itself. As stated in an FPPB contribution to one of *Our Home*'s first issues, "Families consist of people and families make up a nation. If the quality of family life improves, the nation benefits. A country which can control population growth can offer more jobs, better housing and better social services."[10] FPPB partnered with HDB to convey this message until the former was disbanded in 1986. Beyond the vehicle of *Our Home*, FPPB further entrenched its message regarding the merits of family planning through home visits that were targeted specifically at HDB estates.[11] This coupling of these two key government organizations was by no means accidental. The ability to manipulate family size through public housing was initiated by Lee Kuan Yew himself with his 1967 National Day address in which he stated, "We have to revise all our social values so that no one is required to have a large family in order to qualify for a Housing Board flat, for social relief and so on. Today, strange as it may seem, we are giving priority to people with large families, thereby encouraging people to have large families" (quoted in Sun 2012, 63).

Thus, using various policy mechanisms at its disposal, and getting its message out via extensive media campaigns, the PAP "created an atmosphere of crisis and identified large families as an imminent threat to the limited resources of the city-state" in the early years of its rule (Salaff 1988, 21). Then, because the antinatalist policies of the 1960s and 1970s were so effective that the fertility rate fell below replacement level by the early 1980s, the city-state became the first newly industrialized country to adopt pronatalist policies. As Janet Salaff commented shortly thereafter, "Seeing the diminishing gene pool as a threat to the meritocratic-eugenic approach of the political order, the leadership worries that the quality nation's labor pool will dry up" (1988, 261). Indeed, immediately upon making the shift to pronatalism, the eugenicist logic that animated the antinatalist policies—with their emphases on creating a "quality" population by limiting childbirths among low-income women—was even more explicitly brought to the fore in the "Great Marriage Debate." In 1983, Prime Minister Lee Kuan Yew reprimanded the nation's mothers for failing to reproduce themselves along race and class lines in appropriate numbers. He thus encouraged those he referred to as "graduate mothers," that is, women with university educations and belonging disproportionately to the Chinese community, to replace themselves and to discourage poorly educated women of generally Malay or Indian backgrounds from reproducing too freely. Incentives for the former group included "generous tax breaks, medical insurance privileges, and admission for their children to the best schools in the country," while disincentives for the latter group came in the form of cash awards "to restrict their childbearing to two children, after which they would 'volunteer' themselves for tubal ligation" (Heng and Devan 1995, 200). There was much backlash, particularly from the women's movement,[12] and some of Lee Kuan Yew's more contentious claims— such as explicit linkages of race and class and fitness for parenthood, and the call to bring back polygamy for those members of the population who were most "vital"—were tempered. But, the general rationale of encouraging the "right" people to populate the city-state remains to this day, even as low fertility levels continue unabated. Tertiary-educated women were singled out as particular problems and labeled as overly career-minded and too choosy in their choice of partners. From the state's eugenicist perspective, "the loss of their progeny was a loss to the nation's talent pool" (Teo 2010, 339).

In 1986, the Family Planning and Population Unit was replaced with the Population Policy Unit. It set about enacting policies to encourage the educated and economic elite to have many children, while using a combination of incentives and disincentives to encourage everyone else—including those in lower socioeconomic brackets, as well as anyone not in a heterosexual couple—to have fewer. Over the last thirty years, those encouraged to have more children have been able to access tax breaks, housing subsidies, baby bonuses, paid maternity leaves, free medical services such as discounted delivery room fees and publicly provided assisted reproductive treatments, and more; this array of incentives has been deliberately held out of reach of lower income families and divorced or single parents. Disincentives for the latter group include the perpetuation of sterilization schemes, subsidized abortion access, legal prohibition from using assisted reproductive technologies, less government paid maternity leave time, and more (see Lim 1989; Drakakis-Smith et al. 1993; Sun 2012; Teo 2011; Wong et al. 2004). In addition, in 1984 the PAP set up the Social Development Unit, a national matchmaking agency aimed at assisting university graduates to find partners. The Social Development Service was subsequently formed to assist those with lower educational qualifications, and in 2009, as anxieties over the persistent below-replacement fertility level deepened, the two were merged to form the Social Development Unit in a bid to give members a wider pool from which to choose. As Gavin Jones notes, "The efforts of the SDU tended to be scoffed at internationally; locally, there was a certain stigma about being known to be seeking a partner through the government's matchmaking efforts. However, it is widely accepted in Singapore that the demise of earlier traditions of matchmaking, combined with long working hours and limited opportunities to socialize, left a void in possibilities of finding a suitable partner" (2012, 91). The state also promotes proper family formation through frequent public education efforts launched by the Public Education Committee on Family. Its initiatives include marriage preparation workshops and guidebooks, radio and television programming on the value of family, and campaigns like 2003's Romancing Singapore. As Kenneth Paul Tan notes, the campaign "aimed to celebrate 'life, love and relationships' by encouraging heterosexual couples, caught up in fast-paced lifestyles, to 'be more expressive with their partners at all times, not just on special occasions'" (2003, 404–405).

So the family is indeed one of the cornerstones upon which Singapore's post-colonial socioeconomic development has been built, as the PAP made its "upgrading" a key goal in the early years of its governance and has striven to maintain this institution in more recent decades. But what PM Lee did not mention when he made his 2007 speech was that the state still expends considerable efforts to maintain the Singapore family because it still perceives it to be in crisis. Despite the persistence of governmental exhortations to marry and procreate over the last few decades, a significant portion of Singaporeans delay marriage or remain single, and the city-state's fertility rate hovers well below replacement level.[13] Thus the dual demographic trends of declining fertility and an aging population have the contemporary PAP worried about the state of the Singapore family and, in tandem, the future health of the Singapore economy.[14]

It is in this context that the state's continued channeling of resources into the wide variety of measures aimed at encouraging family formation detailed above—from funding a national matchmaking scheme and marriage preparation courses to providing tax incentives for childbirth and extra public housing subsidies for those who live in close proximity to their parents and much more—must be understood. Against the tide, the PAP still appeals to family values. As *Family First: State of the Family Report 2009* states,

> Families today face ever-increasing pressures and demands. Forces such as globalisation, changing family structure and 24/7 connectivity are changing the landscape in which individuals and families operate. Such developments present us with greater options and opportunities, but they also bring about new challenges

and distractions. We are seeing an increase in the number of singles. Singaporeans are getting married and having children later. Couples are having fewer children. Family size is getting smaller. Divorce is increasing. Competing aspirations seem to be affecting marriage and parenthood decisions.

But there is hope, since "overall, the average Singapore family remains strong. The majority of Singaporeans still believe in marriage and want children. They hold pro-family values and attitudes, and enjoy close ties with their family members" (Singapore National Family Council and Ministry of Community Development, Youth and Sports 2009). This is the general PAP line today. The family is a pivotal Singapore institution that remains central within Singaporean's hearts and minds, but it needs continued support to get through these challenging times.

The State of the Singapore Family

Much scholarly work and government discourse laud the PAP's initiatives throughout Singapore's postcolonial period as ones that foster social harmony and responsibility, facilitate the liberation of women, and create the reliable workforce that attracts multinational capital and establishes the foundation for sustained economic growth. In contrast, critics point out the ways in which the family norm in Singapore is a product of PAP ideology that was put in place in ways that produced gender, race, and class biases while disciplining the population. Here, I survey the latter arguments, connecting selected works penned across several decades in order to highlight a common critical impulse over time.

The Singapore state has long been very good at silencing detractors. Thus, the city-state's standard historical narrative tends to be written in narrowly political ways. That is, demographics are depicted as no more than "problems" to be overcome or "explanations" for politicians' failings.[15] But, the initial post-independence changes to Singapore domestic norms occurred within a rich and complicated sociopolitical landscape. In the early years of its rule, the PAP was dealing with social issues alongside and as part of long-standing power struggles with key figures in ethnic and clan associations, communist factions, and student and labor movements. Furthermore, as Gregory Clancey notes in relation to housing reform, a field entangled with family policy reform, "It is perhaps futile to decide whether it was concern for the poor or fear of them which most fueled housing reform. It was clearly both" (2003, 3). Thus the PAP's early reform efforts must be understood as part of this broader context (see Barr and Trocki 2009).

Janet Salaff writes, "Through its new vertical bureaucracy, the state eclipsed many of the long-standing local interest groups on which Chinese society was built, including lineage and clan associations. These heterogeneous guilds, or *hui guan*, drew mainly on family, kin, ethnic, and other parochial allegiances.

Generally based on dialect, they advanced their members' welfare by introducing men to jobs and providing mutual aid, burial, education, and other services" (1988, 20). She continues that the PAP regime "took over such social services, weakened the strong hui guan, and coopted their leaders" (1988, 21). Furthermore, Chua Beng Huat states that while "the monopoly of housing provision has been used to shore up the family institution, which the government has ideologically adopted formally as the 'fundamental' institution of society" (1997, 141), these housing and family policy reforms disrupted multifamily networks and cultural practices, while isolating women to the home where they are solely responsible for homemaking and childcare. Christopher Tremewan similarly argues that the PAP-induced change in household composition strongly affected community relations, particularly within Singapore's various ethnic groups: "Forced resettlement in [Housing Development Board] flats not only split up communities but, as the flats were designed for nuclear families, also split up generations and ensured that the nuclear family became the basic social unit. Thus, HDB residents were moved from an extended family context with an active community life of mutual support and a sense of local identity and security into serried ranks of self-contained concrete boxes" (1994, 50). Furthermore, several scholars discuss the class-based effects of Singapore's family and housing policies, highlighting the ways in which families in the postcolonial city-state were brought into the market economy as the rise of waged work was coupled with expansion of home ownership and formal rental agreements.[16]

Thus, critics of the PAP's early policy initiatives argue that they put in place a family norm that proletarianized the population, curtailed potential for ethnically based activism or electoral challenge, produced an anti-welfarist political economy, and radically transformed gender roles within households in ways that did not necessarily "liberate" women. The postcolonial Singapore family, as such, has done far more than just police a heterosexual-homosexual binary since its inception, and the raced, gendered, and classed logics underpinning it have by no means gone away since the PAP shifted toward pronatalist policies.

In terms of race and class, as noted above, the explicit ties that Lee Kuan Yew tried to make between race, class, and parental fitness were tempered after much public backlash. But the PAP's pronatalist policies since the 1980s have had differential effects on different factions of the city-state's population. The class-based differential effects are obvious and intended, as the emphasis on "elites" versus lower income persons demonstrates. In terms of race, a much more sensitive issue to talk about in Singapore—where multiracialism is enshrined as a core value and freedom of speech on race and ethnicity is extremely curtailed through mechanisms such as the Sedition Act—intentions are difficult to demonstrate. But it is well known that the Malay community is the most socioeconomically disadvantaged community in the city-state, and much scholarship has shown that racial and class discrimination is tied in this case. As

Tania Li writes, "The image of backwardness and its supposed cultural causes have themselves become part of the cultural fabric of Malay and Singapore society, and they have real practical effects as they are incorporated into the daily lives of ordinary Singaporeans and into national political processes" (1989, 167). Writing about the Malay community's state-funded benevolent organization, Mendaki, she continues,

> To improve the standard of education and welfare in the Malay community, [the Mendaki programme] moved beyond the criticism of the values of the "old Malay" and concentrated on promoting the social values, based on Islam, that the leaders felt should characterize the new, successful, Malay. The focus of Mendaki's programme has been the family and through speeches, media coverage, booklets, marriage-guidance courses, sermons in the mosques, and community-level meetings, the effort has been made to instruct the Malay community on the techniques and values that will help them build a stable, happy, and successful Muslim family. (1989, 176)

Reading this example through Michael Barr and Jevon Low's argument that "the Singapore systems of meritocracy and multiracialism are no longer concerned primarily with intercommunal tolerance, as they were until the end of the 1970s, but are aggressive programmes of assimilation of the racial minorities into a Chinese dominated society," we can intuit how the drive to create a "quality" population has effects along racial lines (2005, 162).

Furthermore, feminist scholars have powerfully drawn out the gendered stakes. For instance, You Yenn Teo examines the battery of PAP family-oriented policies aimed at maintaining the "traditional" family. She argues that within the state's neoliberal, anti-welfare framework, the family takes on supreme importance as a social institution. Indeed, she argues, the Singaporean subject is a familial one. Yet the state must reconcile the image that it wishes to project to footloose global capital, of Singapore as a "free market," with its extremely interventionist social policies. In Teo's analysis, it does so through the promulgation of family policies that are in fact gendered policies: "Through its gendered approach toward the family, the Singapore state therefore establishes itself as an agent of change concerned with bringing about economic prosperity while at the same time establishing itself as 'protector' of the people's treasured 'values'" (2007, 424). In contrast to the state discourse of "liberating" women through reforms to the family as a social institution, Teo finds that various policies position women in the primary caregiver roles: "[This produces] their unequal status in the labour market and formal politics, and heightens the odd position of women as being both upholders of family values and threats to the long-term viability of the nation through the 'deviant' behaviour of late marriage and low fertility. Women are encouraged to participate in the formal work force, but they are also admonished to marry, raise families, and perform household responsibilities"

(2007, 424). The Singapore family norm is thus shot through with gender norms in ways that place disproportionate pressure on Singaporean women.[17]

In another strong feminist critique, Geraldine Heng and Janadas Devan take on the infamous "graduate mothers affair" of the 1980s. They take issue with the state's efforts to encourage educated women to have children and to discourage uneducated women from doing so, characterizing the state's justification for these discriminatory policies as follows: "Within a few generations, the quality of Singapore's population would measurably decline, with a tiny minority of intelligent persons being increasingly swamped by a seething, proliferating mass of the unintelligent, untalented, and genetically inferior: industry would suffer, technology deteriorate, leadership disappear, and Singapore lose its competitive edge in the world" (Heng and Devan 1995, 197). This attempt to regulate female sexuality, they quite rightly argue, is simultaneously about class and race: the city-state's "obsession with ideal replication" has led to a national aspiration for "the regeneration of the country's population . . . in such ratios of race and class as would faithfully mirror the population's original composition at the nation's founding moment" (Heng and Devan 1995, 196). They argue that this attempt to engineer the national family, both literally and figuratively, is fundamentally a gender issue insofar as both "actual women" and "other" races and cultures are implicitly feminized: "Women, and all signs of the feminine, are by definition always and already antinational" (Heng and Devan 1995, 209).

In one final example of critical feminist work that takes the idea of the Singapore family to task, Lenore Lyons examines "the ways in which non-reproductively oriented sexualities are excluded from dominant representations of the Singaporean nation" (2004a, np). She argues that the state-perpetuated notion of the family as the foundation of the Singaporean nation creates a number of marginalized groups whose sexual/reproductive practices are cast as abnormal. Gays and lesbians are cast as outsiders, she notes. Equally, many women fall outside the definition of model motherhood: "Some women—notably the less educated—carry a heavier burden as workers. More educated women (particularly the Chinese) are required to perform a stronger role as mothers. The patriarchal family is the only site within which mothering should take place" (Lyons 2004a, np). Furthermore, in a rare move in the literature, she identifies migrant workers as being cast as having "alien sexualities." I deal with this point further below. But, for now, it is worth recounting Lyons's statement that "the state actively uses orientalist discourses about dangerous male sexuality (coded around the 'dark' bodies of construction workers form the Indian sub-continent) and lascivious female sexuality (coded around the bodies of poor rural women from South and Southeast Asia) in debates about immigration and employment" (2004a, np). Lyons concludes that the Singaporean state manages its citizenship regime through a narrow notion of family that reflects a gendered vision that is inflected by dynamics of race/ethnicity, class, and sexuality.

These texts go a long way toward defamiliarizing the notion of the ideal family and opening up possibilities for the interruption and reconfiguration of dominant discourses. Here, I want to build on and extend that disruptive impulse. I want to highlight the fact that although sexuality and gender identity are largely left out of the existing critical literature on the Singapore family, this work still forms a foundation on which a queer critique might be built.

The social dynamics of race, gender, and class come most obviously to the fore in the critical literature on the Singapore family. Thus, patriarchy, racial bias, and capitalism are given explanatory power while heteronormativity is explicitly overlooked. Yet, as I have stated throughout this book, heteronormativity is not simply an expression of the valorization of heterosexuality over homosexuality. Rather, it is a set of gender, race, class, and sexual norms that make particular expressions of heterosexuality seem right. So given that existing critical work on the Singapore family already interrogates three of its four main composite norms, it actually offers insight into crucial parts of the puzzle of heteronormativity in the city-state. While many voices within Singapore's LGBT movement and recent queer Singapore studies work insist that gays and lesbians are not a threat to the family norm and can and ought to be integrated within it (as discussed in chapter 1), the critical literature on the Singapore family in fact offers glimmers of other possible registers of response.

Picking up on this literature, we might thus turn the gaze away from seemingly "abnormal" LGBTs and instead put it onto the norm that makes them seem threatening. In focusing on the composition of the center rather than making a plea for the inclusion of one group on the margins, the reality that heteronormative logics do not only affect gays and lesbians is put into stark relief. Though largely unintentionally, the critical literature on the Singapore family shows that many more than gays and lesbians are rendered "queer" as an effect of the narrow notion of domestic propriety that has taken root in the city-state. So are single persons who are not eligible to buy the public housing flats that house more than 85 percent of the population until after age thirty-five and only in the resale market. So are single mothers who are not entitled to full maternity benefits. So are persons without university educations who are discouraged from having more than two children through a series of financial disincentives. These figures, as well as those within the LGBT community, have been deemed incapable of creating and sustaining a "quality" population. As "queered" figures, all of these are stranded in a state of arrested development, cast as hopeless drags on teleological narratives of *heteronormative* reproduction, and as far less than full participants in visions in Singapore's global city future.

In the next section of this chapter, I move forward a queer critique of the Singapore family that accounts for and is responsible to a wide range of "queered" others by turning to a figure that is ubiquitous within the city-state's contemporary landscape, yet almost completely overlooked in critical Singapore studies literatures on both family and sexuality—the "foreign worker." I highlight this group because, like gay and lesbian issues, immigration issues have been a political hot button in Singapore throughout its creative economy era. While the plights of gays and lesbians and temporary migrant laborers are treated separately in public discourse and activist efforts, assumed to have distinct causes and to require different solutions, I argue that the precariousness experienced by both of these groups in contemporary Singapore is at least in part a function of the heteronormative logic that has guided its developmental project since the late colonial period. For the same neoliberal, creative city project that has facilitated the problematic politics of tolerance toward gays and lesbians also entrenches the marginalization of "foreign workers" in the city-state, as it likewise renders them outside the national family.

Singapore as "Best Home"

The family may well be the "basic building block" of Singapore society. But the fact remains that the strong Singapore state has for some time been up against the reality that the specter of the resurgence of an "abnormal" population looms as the fertility rate remains well below replacement level.[18] This fact is a source of much official anxiety. Despite the PAP's considerable efforts to encourage certain factions of its population to procreate, the state cannot force its citizens to have more babies. Furthermore, the Singapore government faces another major challenge to maintaining its optimum population—outward migration flows. Those "elites" at the top of its "gene pool" are seen as a big part of the "talent" pool that, as discussed in chapter 1, the city-state needs to keep its creative economy afloat. To address their departures, the PAP government puts tremendous resources into casting the city-state as the "best home" for talent. In the 2000s, it set up the Overseas Singaporean Unit and the National Population and Talent Division of the Prime Minister's Office with mandates to find ways to maximize Singaporean "talent," either overseas or in the city-state, for economic growth (see Ho 2009; Ho and Boyle 2015). It tasked its media and communications arms to get the message out, and National Day speeches and rallies have stressed the theme of Singapore as "best home" without fail for well over a decade. My focus here, though, is the fact that in addition to continuing to promote marriage and procreation for (the right) Singaporeans, and encouraging local "talent" to retain ties to the city-state, a new strategy for increasing the population was signaled by PM Lee in his 2006 National Day Rally speech: "If we want our economy to grow, if we want to be strong internationally, then we need a growing population and not just numbers but also talents in every field in Singapore. . . . There are things which we can do as a government in order to open our doors and bring immigrants in. But more importantly as a society, we as Singaporeans, each one of us, we have to welcome immigrants, welcome new immigrants" (Lee 2006).

These few lines signaled a momentous change. While the emphasis here on building "talent" is commensurate with the PAP's longer standing creative city aspirations, the association between "talent" and population growth through immigration represents a striking innovation in government policy, one that the PAP pursues today despite much societal opposition.[19] Consider the following lines from the "Summary and Key Proposals" section of A Sustainable Population for a Dynamic Singapore: Population White Paper:

> Our sustainable population objectives are threefold. First, Singaporeans form the core of our society and the *heart* of our nation. To be a strong and cohesive society, we must have a strong Singaporean core. Second, our population and workforce structure must support a dynamic economy that can steadily create good jobs and opportunities to meet Singaporeans' *hopes* and aspirations. Third, Singapore must continue to be a good *home* with a high quality living environment. (National Population and Talent Division 2013, emphasis original)

The document continues by stating that the PAP will undertake the following actions to achieve objectives 1 and 2: "encourage marriage and parenthood," "remain open to immigration," "enhance integration efforts," "create good jobs for Singaporean core in workforce," and "complement Singaporean core with foreign workforce."

Immigration policies have of course long been a cornerstone of Singapore's economic development plans. Alongside FPPB's efforts to limit family size of the city-state's citizens, migration policy was utilized to create the PAP's desired "quality" Singaporean population. While the predominantly single, male migrant worker composition of Singapore's population as a colonial entrepôt was deemed an impediment to stability and growth, various Aliens Ordinances enacted since 1933 had effectively limited immigration to that which would reunite families in the late colonial period. In the initial independence period, strict controls on the import of foreign workers were enacted as the new city-state "buckled down to the task of nation building" and worked at creating a population of *settled* families in part by defining "fixed categories to incorporate citizens of the nation on the one hand and exclude others as non-citizens, or 'aliens' on the other" (Yeoh 2006, 26). As industrialization gathered steam in the 1970s, immigration controls were relaxed and inflows of unskilled laborers—or what the Singapore government refers to as "foreign workers"—from countries such as the Philippines, Indonesia, Thailand, India, Bangladesh, and Sri Lanka were allowed for. The numbers of such immigrants were small through this decade. Over time, though, flows of "foreign workers" have become increasingly central to Singapore's development efforts. In addition, the transition from a manufacturing-based to a service sector economy in the 1980s initiated an inflow of great numbers of skilled foreign laborers—known in Singapore as "foreign talent."[20] Notably, immigration flows in both categories ("foreign workers" and "foreign talent") were restricted as temporary throughout these periods. What was therefore new in 2006 was the government's turn to "welcoming new immigrants" by encouraging some of them to become Singapore citizens.

Policies unveiled after this 2006 speech concertedly encourage the naturalization of *suitable* immigrants, with suitability determined in direct relation to immigration category. In other words, the potential "new immigrants" are "foreign talent," or "quality people" in the terms used to refer to this group in the 2010 *Making Singapore a Leading Global City* report (Economic Strategies Committee 2010). An information pack produced by the Immigration and Checkpoints Authority (ICA) titled "Embrace Singapore, Where You Belong!" lays out this invitation clearly: "In the embracing spirit of our forebears, we welcome you to our shores, to be part of our country's vitality. . . . Together let's work and contribute to our continued prosperity and shape our future here—our Home." It further directly implores, "Share your talents. Build a nation."[21]

As a result of this shift in policy, the numbers of new permanent residents and citizens in Singapore have risen considerably in the last decade. For my purposes, I highlight that this invitation to naturalization is an offer to join the national family, literally as well as figuratively. The fact that Singapore's government now considers these migrants an essential factor of the city-state's social reproduction is expressed as follows in the same ICA information pack: "Many of you have even brought family members to Singapore to help you better adjust to living here. . . . You and your family members have benefited from what Singapore has to offer, just as Singapore has progressed and prospered with your labour and contributions. It is time to take a step further and become a part of the Singapore family."[22] A dedicated section titled "Dear Family Members" further details "what Singapore has to offer to foreigners and their families." Among the "advantages of living, working and learning in Singapore" laid out here are "a standard of living rated amongst the highest in Asia Pacific and comparable to many first world countries," "the comfortable pace of life, quality education and health care," "the good transport and utilities infrastructure," "and the feeling of safety and security in a country where crime rates are one of the lowest in the world." All of these fruits of Singapore's socioeconomic development to date are offered to "foreign talent" so that they will "help her [Singapore] remain continually relevant to the dynamic and changing environments on the world stage." This linkage between Singapore's future and "foreign talent" is echoed again and again in government discourse in the city-state's current creative economy era. Former prime minister and now minister mentor Lee Kuan Yew has put it most plainly: "Without new citizens and permanent residents, we are going to be the last of the Mohicans. We will disappear" (quoted in *Straits Times* 2009a).

As such, "foreign talent"—particularly those who will form heterosexual families and help reproduce the nation—are cast as harbingers of a bright future and offered a secure place within the city-state. This is significant not least

FIGURE 4.1. Outdoor ad for one of Singapore's many new condo developments marketed to local and foreign "talent." (Photo by author)

because inviting "foreign talent" into Singapore's developmental future opens the carefully crafted Singaporean family up to new members. At the same time, however, this family's borders are reinforced to keep another migrant population, and a much more numerically significant one, out of public life and beyond the pale of public participation. Despite the emphasis in government discourse on bringing "talent" to Singapore, its efforts over the past decade to become a leading creative/global city have been accompanied by a much larger surge of "foreign workers" to the city-state. In 2009, Singapore's foreign population numbered 1.2 million, approximately a quarter of its total population. Within this group, only around 170,000 were expatriate professionals (i.e., "foreign talent"), while the remainder were low-wage "foreign workers" largely in the domestic service and construction sectors (Baey 2010). In contrast to "foreign talent," there are no glossy brochures inviting "foreign workers" into the national family. Rather, they are rendered permanently transient and alien through a range of policies that regulate their time in Singapore. As Brenda Yeoh notes, "Perceived to be potentially disruptive to Singaporean society if left unregulated, state policy is opposed to long-term immigration and directed at ensuring that this category of migrants remains a transient workforce, subject to repatriation during periods of economic downturn" (2006, 29).

Many scholars have offered very useful critiques of the distinctions made between "foreign talent" and "foreign workers" in Singapore and of the different policy frameworks that govern the lives of each group (Kitiarsa 2008; Poon 2009; Teo and Piper 2009; Yeoh and Chang 2001; Yeoh and Huang 2010). The existing literature goes a long way toward explaining the gender, class, and race biases underpinning this bifurcated labor regime. It lays out the ways in which elitism, essentialist notions of multiculturalism, a desire to maintain the racial composition of Singapore's population, and the feminization of low-skilled work are all highly relevant explanatory factors. But, as is also the case in regard to the literatures on family and housing, sexuality is largely absent from critical migration scholarship within Singapore studies. Yet, although very little mention is made in this literature of the sexual regulation of these two groups of migrants as also, and inextricably, central to their differentiation, the exclusion of "foreign workers" is a clearly a function of patriarchal, racialized, elite, and heteronormative cultural logics. For while those migrants who fall under the category "foreign talent" are invited into the national family to help reproduce the nation, those who are characterized as "foreign workers" are excluded from Singapore society and rendered permanently extranational. Crucially, this exclusion is enacted fundamentally through exclusion from the institution of the family and the sphere of social reproduction. As the Employment of Foreign Manpower Act states,

> The foreign employee shall not go through any form of marriage or apply to marry under any law, religion, custom or usage with a Singapore Citizen or Permanent Resident in or outside Singapore. . . . If the foreign employee is a female foreign employee, the foreign employee shall not become pregnant or deliver any child in Singapore during and after the validity of her Work Permit. . . . The foreign employee shall not be involved in any illegal, immoral or undesirable activities, including breaking up families in Singapore. (Singapore Ministry of Manpower 2009)

In other words, "foreign workers" have no future in Singapore. They, like LGBT persons, are considered by the state to be part of Singapore's production but not its social reproduction.

It is important to clarify here that I am certainly not the first to highlight the important role that these prohibitions on marriage and procreation play in constraining the lives of "foreign workers" in the city-state. On the contrary, this section of the Foreign Employees Act is well recognized in the existing literature. But its significance is, I argue, persistently understood only partially. For instance, Angelia Poon argues, "Collectively, the state's many public pronouncements, the Immigration Act, and the regulatory measures for work permit holders regarding marriage and reproduction amount to a bifurcated governmentality that results in the constitution and embodiment of foreign workers and foreign talent in specific racialized and classed ways" (2009, 82). Brenda Yeoh and Shirlena Huang agree that these regulations stem from anxieties around race and nationality and also add gender to the mix. They focus on the ways in which these restrictions on reproduction and marriage lead to popular portrayals of female "foreign workers" as sexual threats, and for this they blame "the highly gendered nature of government immigration policy" (2010, 46). Again, I agree that "foreign worker" policies are products of race, class, gender, and nationality biases. But our analyses are unduly partial unless we also understand these prohibitions as heteronormative. Singapore's "foreign workers" are stranded in a heterotemporality that is queered via regulatory mechanisms that render them permanently transient and outside naturalization (and normalization). They are rendered abject, alien, and, in a non-identarian sense, "queer" as they are deliberately made to exist outside the sphere of intimacy, love, and familial connection—and thus outside the nation.

Two qualifiers to this argument are in order here. First, "foreign workers" in Singapore of course exert agency, and many manage to have sexual lives while in the city-state.[23] Furthermore, they also very often maintain family connections in their home countries. My aim is to stress that their sexual and familial lives are not state sanctioned or supported while in Singapore. Second, I am not suggesting that all migrants are heterosexual. Rather, my point is that the Singapore state presumes them to be and regulates them as such; and in part through the regulation of their sexual/familial/reproductive lives, migrant workers are excluded from Singapore's progress narrative. While those migrants who fall under the "foreign talent" category are cast as harbingers of a bright future for the city-state, the "foreign workers" are cast as only supplemental to Singapore's national development. They are rendered as anachronistic because they do the jobs that Singaporeans *no longer* want to do. They are cast as only productive and not reproductive, and the ways in which the Singapore state coerces and constrains the mobility of "foreign workers" lead to lives lived asynchronously and out of place in this forward-looking global city.

To reinforce this point, I close this section by returning to housing policy, and specifically to citizenship, the final factor in determining eligibility for HDB tenancy beyond age and family composition. Ownership of flats is limited to Singapore citizens and permanent residents, while foreigners legally residing in the city-state may rent or sublet housing flats with one significant exception— foreign construction workers.[24] This group must be housed in dormitories provided by their employers, and it is this fact that led to a national controversy in 2008 when residents of Serangoon Gardens, an affluent private housing estate of semidetached bungalows, terrace houses, and low-rise condominiums, presented a petition to the government in objection to a plan to convert an unused former school into a dormitory for foreign workers. The concerns raised by the residents centered around assertions that housing workers in the unused school would lead to higher crime rates, an unclean environment, changes to the character of the neighborhood, and conflicts between Singaporeans and foreign workers due to "cultural differences."

FIGURE 4.2. Serangoon Gardens foreign worker dormitory. (Photo by author)

Despite much public criticism over this display of xenophobia in the pages of Singapore's daily newspapers and on the blogs of prominent local social and political commentators, the Ministry of National Development made a series of concessions to accommodate the disgruntled residents. These included the expansion of the "buffer zone" between the dormitory and existing residences, the construction of a separate access road, and requirements that the dormitory management work with the police to implement security measures and that they also provide house rules "to minimize disturbances to the neighbourhood" (see figure 4.2). There is much to be said about this conflict over neighborhood development, but here I draw attention to one thread of the debate that has not yet been brought to the fore. The fact that the workers to be housed were all male and without families came up again and again in the public statements made by the residents, especially in response to criticisms that the residents welcome "foreign talent" but not "foreign workers." As one commentator on the *Straits Times* forum page put it, "The expats arrive here with their families and they put their children in schools here. Foreign workers are in a 'bachelor' state without their family. They are grouped together, single men in dormitories. The situation is entirely different. The connotations emanating from foreign single men living in dorms in an estate which is predominantly family-oriented is only too obvious."[25] The author need not say any more because, even though the state purports that the Singapore family is "in crisis," familial and domestic norms are so well entrenched in contemporary Singapore that their boundaries appear to be plain and right to many.

From Reform to Resistance

Again, Singapore LGBTs' general position that sexual minorities are not a threat to the Singapore family norm and can and ought to be integrated within it is a commonsense and strategic position. It is also a bold one coming from a relatively small and new movement that is given only limited room in which to move within a highly constrained civil society. Though Singapore is now a "creative city," the city-state's government is certainly still a strong and conservative one. But even though avenues for advocacy are curtailed, as the struggle continues, I want to at least table other lines of queer critique and thereby take advantage of the fertile ground of the "gay debates" in Singapore to advance a queer critique. So in this chapter, my aim has been to further push the discussion in another direction, by turning the gaze away from seemingly "abnormal" LGBTs and putting it on the norm that keeps them out of place and time in contemporary Singapore.

The Singapore family is, as the PAP asserts, a core notion on which the city-state's postcolonial socioeconomic development has been built. But this notion is far from fixed. It is the product of ceaseless shaping and reshaping, as shown in the brief account of the postcolonial government's interventions into domestic life in the city-state provided above. Furthermore, it does not go unchallenged. Existing critical scholarship points out its ideological basis and contests its political ends. Queer critique has been largely absent from this body of work to date, unfortunately, with authors making no more than occasional mention of the heterosexist basis of the Singapore family. Yet there are connections to be made. For in calling out the raced, classed, and gendered underpinnings of the Singapore family norm, the existing critical literature extends our understanding of the nature and extent of heterosexual privilege in the city-state. It shows, in other words, that the proper Singapore subject is not heterosexual. It is a specific heterosexual subject who fits in to state-derived notions of proper domesticity.

As I have stressed throughout, the debates around the place of homosexuality in the city-state tend to hone in on problematizing the dividing line between homosexuality and heterosexuality. But when we focus on the family, highlighting its production over time and attending to the ways in which much is cast as foreign to the domestic in Singapore (as everywhere else), the multiplicity of heterosexual subjectivity becomes apparent. *The* Singaporean heterosexual multiplies into single parents, divorced couples, Malay families, "foreign workers," and many other "others."

From Queer to Decolonized

The sexual is spatial and the spatial is sexual. Queer studies scholars, and especially the geographers and urbanists among them, have demonstrated the veracity of this claim for decades. There is now a large literature on the relationship between cities and LGBT movements, subcultures, and everyday lives, and this body of work has grown increasingly nuanced over time. As such, much contemporary scholarship considers "queer spaces" such as "gay villages" and pride events in cities as not simply counterpoints to a predominant urban "straight space" but as spaces that are simultaneously sexualized, raced, classed, gendered, and more (e.g., Andersson 2015; Goh 2018; Hanhardt 2013; Livermon 2012; Misgav and Johnston 2014; Moussawi 2018). This is a logical change. If, as so much queer theory tells us, there is no inherent, biological, a priori sexuality but only a multitude of sexual subjects who come into being through worldly discourse and practice, then there cannot be an essential, uniform, and universally radical queer space. Rather, LGBT spaces in cities and everywhere else are provisional, relational, and geographically and historically contingent spaces. They can be sites of solace, creativity, and progressive politics to be sure, but they can also be sites of exclusion, abjection, and boundary maintenance. There is thus certainly a need for critical analyses of urban LGBT spaces that help us understand queer cultural politics as contested sites in which racializations, genderings, and classed processes take place. But there is also a need to go beyond the notion of "queer space" as "LGBT space" and to read the whole city and all its citizens and subjects as living in a heteronormative time and place. I have read Singapore in such a way in this book. In these final pages, I first rehearse the book's main claims and contentions and then turn to discuss how decentering queer claims to and on space in the city-state can help center a much-needed project of decolonization in Singapore and beyond.

After Queer Space

"There is space," PM Lee told LGBT activists when he refused their request to repeal Section 377A of the Penal Code, "and there are limits." So once a year, a Pink Dot is formed in Singapore. In the context of the dawning of a remarkable but woefully limited era of tolerance within the city-state, LGBT Singaporeans and their supporters push for more room. They enjoy the newfound opportunity to build community openly while making a statement that equity is still a long way off. They call courageously for the "freedom to love." But love's regulation is not only identarian. The relentlessly forward-looking postcolonial Singapore government "stays behind" on the issue of LGBT human rights not just because it seeks to protect an abstract heterosexuality from an encroaching LGBT threat, but also because it is set in its developmental ways. As Jasbir Puar states, "The claiming of space—any space, even the claiming of queer space—[is] a process informed by histories of colonization, these histories operating in tandem with the disruptive and potentially transgressive specifics at hand" (2002, 936). The case of Singapore clearly exemplifies this point. Section 377A of the city-state's Penal Code, the most visible and powerful statement of LGBT exclusion in Singapore, was introduced late in its colonial period. Though put in place to address the colonial administration's anxieties about male same-sex sexual activities, this law was set down on a landscape that was already shot through with heterosexist as well as racist, sexist, nationalist, and elitist biases, biases that come together in powerful and consequential ways around familial and domestic norms consolidated in the late colonial and early postcolonial period. These norms persist in the present day as the PAP government continues to tie notions of the island nation's success, prosperity, and even continued existence to the continuation of a proper domestic/intimate sphere. Along the way, colossal state-based efforts to create a "quality" population through the fostering of a specific Singaporean family norm went ahead. Through these, many more than LGBT persons are rendered out of place and time as the city-state invests in an exclusionary politics of reproductive futurism.

Thus, while the drive to make Singapore a place "in which all Singaporeans are free to love and be loved" is an understandable and useful one, it is only a partial response to Singapore's inequitable intimate politics.[1] For "love" does not exist outside the political. It does not exist outside postcolonial or neoliberal power relations, especially in a context such as Singapore in which the notion of family has so much reach and where that notion hinges on the placement of a specific sort of romantic couple at its core. As Elizabeth Povinelli (2006) argues, "the intimate couple" is a "key transfer point" for logics of governance. More pointedly, as a migrant worker named as Mr. Dulal pointedly states in a rare sympathetic article in Singapore's mainstream local press on the difficulties that "foreign workers" experience locally due to their enforced existence outside the sphere of the family, "Singapore love is all bluff bluff one!"[2] Since the "freedom to love" in Singapore is not curtailed only on the basis of the sex of one's intimate partner, even if LGBT people gain the privilege of marching side by side toward "progress" with Singapore's families through successful struggles for sexual citizenship, their place in the center will rely on an orbit of other "queer" others. To clarify, I am not suggesting that because heteronormativity encompasses not just the sexual but also the racial, the classed, the gendered, and more, all those who are cast as illicit and improper subjects are therefore "queer" in the identarian sense of the term. I am instead arguing that we ought to pay critical attention to the fact that many more than LGBT persons are "queered" in the sense that they are put on a different trajectory of life and death than those cast as licit and proper through the maintenance of narrow familial and domestic norms. We must therefore attend not just to the deployment of "queer" as an identity category but to the process of "queering" that results from heteronormative governance.

Once we go beyond the single issue, it becomes apparent that a queer response must encompass struggles for LGBT rights while also embracing other social struggles in the city-state. Migrant advocacy organizations already focus attention on the deeply important issues of employment standards and humane treatment of "foreign workers." But never is the enforced single status of migrant workers or their perpetual exclusion from naturalization ever raised as issues for debate; and they ought to be since there can be no radical queer future until no lives are deferred. As José Muñoz powerfully states, "The 'should be' of utopia, its indeterminacy and its deployment of hope, stand against capitalism's ever expanding and exhausting force field of how things 'are and will be'" (Muñoz 2009, 99). There is an urgent need to denaturalize such a force field in Singapore, to initiate a language of "should" in the face of teleological developmental narratives on numerous fronts in the name of social justice.

Again, I am cognizant of the very real limits placed on activist and other civil society organizations in Singapore. Pink Dot's stance that it has "no agenda but love" may well be as far as it can go right now,[3] and it may be wise for locally based organizations to continue to publicly raise the concerns of migrant workers, and women, and low-income or split families, and LGBT people in silo-like fashion, leaving the connections between these issues in the background and thus sidelining the possibility of advancing more radical demands on the state. After all, as those familiar with recent Singapore history will know, the "Aware Saga"—which nearly brought down the city-state's longest standing women's activist organization on the grounds that it had a "homosexual agenda" merely because it promoted a sex education program that did not condemn same-sex activity—is still fresh in local imaginations (see Chong 2013). But we can begin to think about sexual and gender identity politics differently and to build a new archive of more broadly encompassing critical scholarship on which those working at the state-civil society nexus can draw. Much work within the strong and ever-expanding corpus of critical Singapore studies is already advancing potentially narrative-changing critiques of the PAP's economic and social policies. Most notably, calls to turn away from development strategies that yield economic growth at the cost of increased societal inequalities and to instead embrace welfarism are gaining ground (see Teo 2018), as are calls for a deepening of democratic norms in the city-state (see George 2017). As noted in previous chapters, there is now more room in Singapore to express desires for other paths than at any other point in its postcolonial era, and this room is being filled in all kinds of creative and promising ways. "Queering" the dominant Singapore success story by at once responding to its homophobia and transphobia *and* critiquing the broader politics of intimacy of which these ills are part can and ought to be a central part of the process of arriving at alternative visions; and, crucially, attending to Singapore as a heteronormative space affirms the need for these alternate visions to be explicitly decolonizing ones.

As noted in the introduction, much urban scholarship has moved away from thinking narrowly about the "global city" as a category or thing to instead critically examine the "worlding" of cities as a process. As such, there are existing but so far largely untapped solidarities between urban studies and queer studies. Within urban studies, deployments of "worlding" as a conceptual and analytical tool argue productively for a provincializing of urban theory, in the postcolonial theoretical sense. As Jennifer Robinson notes, to decolonize the field of urban studies, "theoretical reflections should at least be extremely clear about their limited purchase and even better, extend the geographical range of empirical resources and scholarly insight for theorizing beyond the West and western-dominated forms of globalization" (2006, 549). As critical urban scholars expand their purview as they try to envision ways to "world" cities differently, queer critique can and ought to be engaged with as a mode of alternate world making. As Lauren Berlant and Michael Warner state,

> By queer culture we mean a world-making project, where "world," like "public," differs from community or group because it necessarily includes more people than can be identified, more spaces than can be mapped beyond a few reference points, modes of feeling that can be learned rather than experienced as a birthright. The queer world is a space of entrances, exits, unsystematized lines of acquaintance, projected horizons, typifying examples, alternate routes, blockages, incommensurate geographies. (1998, 558)

Beyond highlighting the need to take the lives and concerns of sexual and gender minorities seriously within global urban studies and the need to take the urban dimensions of global queer politics seriously within queer studies, we can bring together the worlding projects of both queer studies and urban studies. We can harness the compatible utopian impulses of both fields, impulses that have heretofore been advanced largely in parallel.

Unsettling the Global City

On January 4, 2018, the *Guardian* published an opinion piece titled "Colonialism Can Work—Just Look at Singapore." Its thumbnail description states, "The country's postcolonial rulers seized the advantages left them by the British empire and used them, for the most part, for the benefit of wider society." The author hails Singapore as a "rich country" with excellent schools and housing and calls it "the best of both worlds: a place where Asian cultural traditions remain intact but western know-how is harnessed to build a prosperous society." Toward the end of the piece, the author notes that "the Singapore story also shows us the price societies pay when their rulers make use of the tools colonial authorities left behind" and lists a "chilling climate for free speech," the absence of independent trade unions, and a lack of space for opposition politics as some of the costs. Then, with no urging to address these serious issues, the piece concludes with the simple assertion that Singapore is a model for development because it is a "paternalist state." "Western rule is not required, as Singapore shows, only an openness to modern ideas—which in the future, will not always come from the west." The piece is, frankly, facile clickbait.[4] Yet it cannot be easily dismissed. Though condensed and reductive, it parrots Singapore state discourse. The curtailing of some civil liberties is a small price to pay for efficiency, modernity, and affluence, the PAP avers, while it celebrates the city-state's colonial past as a stepping stone to its postcolonial, modern, economically successful present.

Furthermore, the many scholars, policy makers, and urban and national governments that laud the PAP's achievements and desire the exportation and geographical extension of the "Singapore model" tacitly embrace this line of thinking. But there is also critical pushback, and a queer reading of the city-state can help bolster it. As Philip Holden states, "If they can work together, critical analysis of colonialism and queer theory surely provide us with the means to assess the extent to which we, and others connected to us by various filiations of identification and power, experience in different ways and to different degrees the condition of living in liberation without freedom" (2003, 317).

Holden does not expand specifically on how queer theory and colonial critique might productively come together in relation to Singapore, but he does write in general terms about Singapore as a postcolonial object of study. He argues that Singapore's "post-colonialism" is not a form of "neo-colonialism," "because in Singapore at present the 'West' can no longer constitute a discrete object of critique." Neither, he continues, is Singapore's "post-colonialism" "simply an extension of colonialism," for "Singapore is not a colonial power." Yet Singapore's colonial past must still be critically dealt with, he argues, for it lingers in the present in ways that are "willfully effaced from Singapore's national narrative" (2008, 351). There is a need, in the first instance, to employ a postcolonial critique that can do the work of "remembering otherwise," thus bringing suppressed and ignored voices to the fore (Holden 2008, 351) while being mindful to avoid "a certain kind of nostalgia for a past that one has never known, a retelling of narratives in which those forgotten by history now become romantic protagonists with whom the contemporary researcher identifies" (2008, 352). In addition, Holden advocates a "second form of postcolonial analysis in Singapore," one that aims to highlight "different forms of colonialism that haunt the present" (2008, 353). He states, "The 'post-colonial'—the sudden presence of a colonial shadow in a present from which we have been told all such shadows have been banished—carries a certain heuristic power" (2008, 353). He argues, in other words, for the importance of approaching social justice issues in the city-state with a postcolonial approach that reconfigures, interrupts, and defamiliarizes its present and thus challenges the powerful teleological narratives of progress and development that have long guided its trajectory.

In the broad field of critical Singapore studies, some scholarship advances such a postcolonial approach explicitly and fulsomely. For instance, in his work on housing in postcolonial Singapore, historian Loh Kah Seng (2009, 2007) take pains to draw out the continuities between the colonial and postcolonial administrations' approaches to social policies and programs. Another historian, Timothy Harper (2001, 1997), foregrounds the lost internationalist connections that various Singapore communities maintained during the late colonial period, as a counterpoint to the narrow notion of cosmopolitanism that animates contemporary global city Singapore. Yet most critical Singapore studies scholarship does not seriously or concertedly grapple with colonial legacies. As Harper notes, "Much of the literature on Singapore has emerged from within the nation-building project. The tensions and paradoxes within Singapore's identity are largely spoken of as something new: something born out of the events of 1965, and fortified by an ethic of survival in the face of new global pressures. Rarely are these tensions viewed from the prospect of Singapore's past. If they have a history, it is a legacy *from* the colonial period, rather than *of* it" (1997, 262). This is a crucial observation. The question "whose city/nation is Singapore?" implicitly animates critical Singapore studies. Concerns over the ways that elitist, patriarchal, racist, nationalist, and heterosexist dynamics play out in the city-state have given rise to much important work on the plights of women, the poor, migrants, LGBT people, ethnic minorities, youth, the elderly, and more. Furthermore, this scholarship seeks to bring alternative global city futures into view. But time is not linear. It folds and bends and re-turns and, as such, "many areas of contemporary social contention in the city-state have colonial associations or lineages" (Holden 2008, 358). Thus, to foster a future in which all Singaporean citizens and residents can safely and comfortably dwell and thrive, historical dislocations must be taken seriously.

Over the years that I have spent working on this book, I have come back to this quote from Lauren Berlant again and again:

How many times have I asked my own students to explain why, when there are so many people, only one plot counts as "life" (first comes love, then . . .)? Those who don't or can't find their way in that story—the queers, the single, the something else—can become so easily unimaginable, even often to themselves. Yet it is hard not to see lying about everywhere the detritus and the amputations that come from attempts to fit into the fold; meanwhile, a lot of world-building energy atrophies. (1998, 286)

Slightly later in the same text, she states, "What kind of (collective, personal) future can be imagined if, for example, sexuality is no longer bound to its narrative" (1998, 287). In relation to the Singapore case, I have sought to answer Berlant's question about why "only one plot counts as 'life'" by unbounding sexuality from the dominant Singapore story. This is not, I have argued, a case of a modern forward-thinking city-state that just is not quite ready to offer rights to LGBT persons. Rather, it is a case of postcolonial/settler city-state with a long and continuing history of intervening in the private/domestic/intimate lives of its population. As such, even if policy and legislative changes geared to easing the discrimination and biases that LGBT persons face daily in Singapore are eventually put in place, queering/abjection/exclusion will not cease. There is thus a pressing need to do the work of challenging the confining urban/national imaginaries that render so many people "unimaginable, even often to themselves."

As Zhang, Wu, and Yeoh note, "The Singaporean rationality is to put everyone in their 'rightful place' according to carefully calibrated visions and plans" (2015, 236). True to form, the world-renowned effective and efficient Singapore state does this work well. So there is, in Berlant's terms, much "detritus" and atrophied "world-building energy." Many lifeworlds have been ruined in post/colonial Singapore. For instance, though LGBT subcultures flourish in the present-day city-state, many people undoubtedly stay away from them due to fears of reprisal and rejection. Or consider the lives of past and present migrants to the city-state and the ways the Singapore state confines and contains their movements in public and private. Or take the ethnic and clan associations that have been forever disrupted by state housing and multiculturalism policies and programs. But remember that atrophy is not necessarily waste and that suppression of alternate notions of kinship, nation, community, and citizenship is not natural but politically produced. Singapore is both a "gay-friendly" but determinedly unqueer and a postcolonial but not decolonized city-state. But its future can be pried open, and thinking beyond identity politics to acknowledge and build on connections across axes of difference must be a vital part of such a project.

NOTES

Introduction

1. Lee Hsien Loong, National Day Rally speech, NUS University Cultural Centre, August 21, 2005.

2. Pink Dot print ad, "Come make Pink Dot 16.05.09," www.pinkdotsg.blogspot.com.

3. Promotional video, "Come Make Pink Dot: 18 June 2011," www.pinkdotsg.blogspot.com.

4. For recent migrant numbers to Singapore, see Ministry of Manpower, "Foreign Workforce Numbers," http://www.mom.gov.sg/documents-and-publications/foreign-workforce -numbers.

5. Employers of Foreign Domestic Workers in Singapore have been legally required to provide them with one day off per week only since 2013.

6. "From third world to first" is a phrase first popularized in relation to Singapore as the title of one of Lee Kuan Yew's memoirs (Lee 2000).

7. For more on Singapore's role as a model for urban and national development, see Chua (2011), King and Idawati (2010), Moser (2012), Lee and Hwang (2012), Pow (2014), and Zhang (2012). On how Singapore's government actively markets and exports its expertise, see the Economic Strategies Committee (2010).

8. See, for instance, the GaWC rankings of "global cities" since 2000 at http://www .lboro.ac.uk/gawc/gawcworlds.html or the Mori Institute's (Japan) new Global City Power Index at http://mori-m-foundation.or.jp/english/ius2/gpci2/index.shtml.

9. See the film *To Singapore with Love*, directed by Tan Pin Pin, which includes interviews with political exiles from Singapore and was banned from screening in the city-state by the PAP government in September 2014.

10. On this point, see Oswin (2008).

Chapter 1. A Developmental City-State

1. Transcribed from a video of Lee's remarks available at https://www.youtube.com/watch ?v=JbOKJhiuH5Y&list=PL9Qs1H4CimXbNp8WRbm-J6VtVOH5oNwOa&index=1.

2. As Olds and Yeung note, "Postcolonial political dynamics (esp., the 1965 ejection of Singapore from Malaysia) concentrated the minds of politicians on the necessity of pursuing the global city pathway years before academics and planners were speaking of the 'global city' or the 'world city'" (2004, 510). Indeed, long before John Friedmann (1986), Saskia Sassen (1991), and others began to articulate scholarly understandings of the "global city," the ambitious postcolonial government of the Southeast Asian city-state of Singapore was self-consciously trying to create one. Consider the following description of Singapore as a global city from an address explicitly titled "Singapore: Global

City" that S. Rajaratnam made to the Singapore Press Club in 1972 in his capacity as foreign minister. In the context of discussing appraisals of Singapore's prospects as a nation-state at the time of its separation from Malaysia, he reflected, "The pessimistic scenario was written on the assumption that an independent Singapore would be a self-contained city state; that it would, at the most, be a regional city and therefore its fate and fortunes would depend wholly on the economic climate of the region. The economic climate of the region is no doubt important to us and what happens in the region would have consequences for us economically, politically and militarily. But we are more than a regional city. We draw sustenance not only from the region but also from the international economic system to which as a Global City we belong and which will be the final arbiter of whether we prosper or decline" ([1972] 1977, 19).

3. In 1981, Lee Kuan Yew stated that a wealthy nation "cannot carry health, unemployment and pension benefits without massive taxation and overloading the system, reducing the incentives to work and to save and care for one's family—when all can look to the state for welfare. . . . Social and health welfare are like opium or heroin. People get addicted, and withdrawal of welfare benefits is very painful" (quoted in Barr 2003, 84).

4. Eligibility requirements for the purchase of subsidized Housing Development Board flats are virtually unchanged today (see www.hdb.gov.sg). The applicant must be twenty-one years of age and "form a proper family nucleus," which is defined as the applicant and fiancé(e); the applicant, spouse, and children (if any); the applicant, the applicant's parents, and siblings (if any); if widowed/divorced, the applicant, and children under the applicant's legal custody; and, if orphaned, the applicant and unmarried siblings.

5. As Chua observes, "The selection of English as effectively the national lingua franca helps in significant ways to shore up the ideological underpinnings of economic competition among individual citizens. As a foreign tongue, English is arguably 'ethnically neutral' and has to be learned by every Asian person." The official logic is, therefore, that "achievement in English competency can therefore be attributed to the hard work plus natural endowment of the individual, i.e. to one's own merit, thus generating a meritocratic system" (2010, 340). On a related point, see Ho (2012) for an excellent critical analysis of the ways in which the Singapore education system's stratification of students into distinct educational tracks is tied to hierarchical citizenship roles for "elite" and "nonelite" students.

6. On this point, Michael Barr notes, "Lee Kuan Yew left Singapore with a legacy of ethnic silos: so that matters of race and ethnicity could be addressed only within a conceptual and institutional framework based rigidly on racial divides. Indians turned to SINDA; Chinese to the Chinese Development Assistance Council (CDAC). Malays turned to MENDAKI, or to its non-government rival, AMP" (2003, 80).

7. See Tan (2012) for a critique of the "Shared Values" that argues for the importance of individual human rights and of public participation in governmental processes.

8. For more on making Singapore the "best home for talent" through urban "place management," see the *Report of the Subcommittee on Making Singapore a Leading Global City*. It states, "We must be the best home for talent—a vibrant global city that embraces a rich diversity of talent and ideas. This will be achieved by offering the best career and

developmental opportunities for Singaporeans and diverse talents, fostering a deep sense of inclusion, connection and commitment to Singapore, and building extensive talent networks between Singapore and the rest of the world" (Economic Strategies Committee 2010).

9. For discussions of the urban transformations that have accompanied Singapore's new economy, see Goh (2001), Teo and Kong (1997), Pow (2011, 2002), Wang (2012), Wong and Bunnell (2006), Yap (2013).

10. It is worth pointing out that Florida's "gay index" has come under much scrutiny. As David Bell and Jon Binnie (2004, 1817) note, Florida relies on census data on gays and lesbians in same-sex partnerships to make his linkage between the presence of "gays" and "creativity," and "the gay index is therefore an index of respectability, of nicely gentrified neighbourhoods." Furthermore, they argue that the incorporation of "sexual others" into entrepreneurial urban governance strategies of place promotion "is a powerful component of the 'new homonormativity'" (1818; see also Manalansan 2005; Rushbrook 2002).

11. For details and critical commentary on these changes, see Tan (2007b) and Yao (2007).

12. Speech to the National Day Rally in 1986, quoted in the *Straits Times,* April 20, 1987; see BBC, "In Quotes: Lee Kuan Yew," http://www.bbc.com/news/world-asia-31582842.

13. Transcribed from a video of Jacobs's remarks available at http://www.asianurbanlab .org/video-singapore-dreaming-conference-jane-m-jacobs/.

14. See the book that emerged from the conference proceedings: Wee and Chia (2016).

15. Quote taken from conference website, http://www.asianurbanlab.org/singapore -dreaming-conference/about-singapore-dreaming-conference/.

Chapter 2. Singapore as "Straight Space"

1. Pink Dot 2012 campaign video, http://pinkdot.sg/someday-directors-note-2/.

2. See People Like Us website, "History" section, www.plu.sg/society/.

3. For an overview of media control in Singapore, see George (2012).

4. See also *Straits Times* (2003a, 2003b).

5. Queer theorists have critically responded to this sort of politics of incorporation. Lisa Duggan coined the term "homonormativity" to describe "a politics that does not contest dominant heteronormative assumptions and institutions, but upholds and sustains them, while promising the possibility of a demobilized gay constituency and a privatized, depoliticized gay culture anchored in domesticity and consumption" (2003, 50). For existing work that brings critiques of homonormativity into conversation with urban studies, see Bell and Binnie (2004), Hubbard (2011, chap. 7), Manalansan (2005), and Oswin (2015).

6. On this point, see, for instance, Bell and Binnie (2004), Cohen (1997), Eng (2005), Manalansan (2005), and Puar (2007).

7. The Remaking Singapore Committee was a governmental committee formed in February 2002 that worked alongside the Economic Review Committee. Both committees were tasked with developing strategies that would take Singapore successfully into the twenty-first century. The Remaking Singapore Committee conducted broad public consultations and thus had a very high public profile.

8. Technically, Section 377 was repealed and reenacted. The subheading "Unnatural Offences" was removed and replaced with "Sexual Penetration of a Corpse" as the statute was rewritten to prohibit necrophilia. In addition, the new sections 377B, C, and D were added to the Penal Code. These deal with bestiality and the definition of terms such as "penetration," "sex," "sexual activity," and sexual offences in cases of "mistake as to age."

9. The full section reads, "Any male person who, in public or private, commits, or abets the commission of, or procures or attempts to procure the commission by any male person of, any act of gross indecency with another male person, shall be punished with imprisonment for a term which may extend to 2 years." The statute was added to the Straits Settlements Penal Code in 1938 and has remained in Singapore's Penal Code throughout the postcolonial period.

10. While Lee's position on the matter can be read as the official ruling People's Action Party stance, it should be noted that debates over homosexuality in Singapore of the last several years have seen the advancement of a wide variety of positions by non-PAP politicians, scholars, activists, and concerned citizens alike. However, debates over the fate of Penal Code Section 377A were particularly polarized. While an impressive repeal campaign was mobilized, it faced a strong wave of political and popular support for retention of the clause, and the Penal Code Amendment Bill passed by an overwhelming majority in Parliament.

11. For an excellent analysis of the politics of tolerance, see Wendy Brown's *Regulating Aversion: Tolerance in the Age of Identity and Empire* (2008). In this book, Brown surrenders an "understanding of tolerance as transcendent or universal concept, principle, doctrine and virtue so that it can be considered instead as a political discourse and practice of *governmentality* that is historically and geographically variable in purpose, content, agents, and objects" (2008, 4, emphasis original). Granting that intolerance is no alternative, she is not *against* tolerance but rather seeks to make plain its depoliticizing, regulatory, and imperialist tendencies and argues for the necessity of critiquing its deployments.

12. Alex Au, "Repeal: A Well-Fought Campaign with Huge Gains," originally posted on fridae.com, reposted at http://archive.globalgayz.com/asia/singapore/gay-singapore -news-and-reports-2/#article19a.

13. Promotional video, "Come Make Pink Dot: 18 June 2011," www.pinkdotsg.blogspot.ca.

14. Pink Dot print ad, "Come make Pink Dot 16.05.09," www.pinkdotsg.blogspot.ca.

15. Alex Au, "Singapore Needs to Think about Gay Marriage Now," *Yawning Bread*, March 2004, http://www.yawningbread.org/arch_2004/yax-365.htm.

16. People Like Us, "Media Release: Government Should Repeal Both Sections 377 and 377A of the Penal Code" (2006), http://www.plu.sg/society/?p=63.

17. For a full discussion of the ways in which LGBT activists have adapted to the constraints of Singapore's political and legal systems, see Chua (2012).

Chapter 3. Section 377A and the Colonial Trace

1. There is no equivalent provision for women, but same-sex relations between neither men nor women receive any legal recognition.

2. Transcript of MP Hri Kumar's 2007 speech to Parliament on Section 377A of the Penal Code, available at http://theonlinecitizen.com/2007/10/section-377a-is-inconsistent -pap-mp-hri-kumar/.

3. For an expression of this position that predates the Penal Code reform debates but nonetheless reflects their tone, see Chua (2003).

4. Frederick Cooper and Ann Laura Stoler's *Tensions of Empire: Colonial Cultures in a Bourgeois World* (1997) is an important edited collection that brings together work demonstrating how imperial governance was not simply imported to and imposed on the colonies but entailed a complex interrelationship between colony and metropole, colonized and colonizer.

5. See also Harper (1997), Hirschman (1986) and Yao (1999).

6. On this point, see Lam and Tan (1999).

7. In particular, Arondekar critiques the use of colonial archives to historicize and universalize "largely Western models of male homosexuality." As evidence of this tendency, she cites Bleys (1995).

8. Manderson (1996) also notes that some colonial officials held that "unnatural vice" was the "lesser sin," quoting Reverend W. G. Shellabear as follows: "It seems to me more horrible for wicked men to ruin innocent young girls than that wicked men should ruin each other." But this was a minority view.

9. The postcolonial government's considerable efforts to create a "Singapore family" for national development as well as their treatment within the substantial archive of Singapore studies scholarship are scrutinized in chapter 4. Through this chapter, I highlight the ways in which this chapter's work of reperiodizing the emergence of the "Singapore family" to the colonial period influences the way we read the postcolonial governance of intimacy in Singapore.

10. Not incidentally, the colonial era sodomy law that contemporary LGBT activists tried unsuccessfully to repeal in 2007 was instituted in 1938. For a fuller discussion of new modes of governing in Singapore's late colonial and early postcolonial periods, see Loh (2013).

11. This treatment of Malay labor is common within colonial discourse. In another example from an annual report section on "Local Malay Labour," it is stated, "Local Malay Labour in the colony is not of importance. The Malays are not as a rule anxious to earn more than is sufficient to support them" (Straits Settlements 1924, 361; also see Hirschman 1986).

12. "Report of the Population Study Group" (Singapore 1955b, 16); and for specific sex ratios by ethnic group as well as a wider discussion of their colonial management, see Levine (1999).

13. There were of course dissenting views on the "abnormal" sex ratio among the colonizers. The following quote is an example of one colonial officer's stark disagreement with the dominant position: "Female immigration should be encouraged by our Government to prevent, if for no other reason, the fearful crimes that prevail amongst the Chinese in consequence of the paucity of females. They exceed all belief and may not be placed in all their repulsiveness before the public. The introduction of women would materially conduce to the peacefulness of the Colony. The Chinese are naturally domesticated, and would, surrounded by their wives and children seek to maintain order and peace; and would not be easily roused as they now are with no ties to restrain them, to side with one faction or another in the event of a quarrel taking place between them" (Vaughan [1879] 1971).

14. UK National Archives, CO 659/13, Letter from Government House, Singapore to Colonial Office, November 14, 1939.

15. For a treatment of the regulation of prostitution in colonial Singapore as well as a compelling social-historical account of the lives of Singapore's prostitutes as a group of marginalized workers, see Warren (2003).

16. UK National Archives, CO 564/1, *First Report of the Advisory Committee on Social Hygiene*, August 1925.

17. Here Loh builds on Harper (1998).

18. Furthermore, Levine critically notes, "Officials, however, did not always connect the conditions they found so offensive with the overwhelming poverty of a working-class Chinese population for whom over-crowding and grime were chronic problems. Instead, they attributed the realities of economic hardship—the result of rapid modernization—to racial traits that were linked to moral failings" (1999, 41).

19. The Straits Chinese elites were of course only one group of colonized elites. I focus in the rest of the chapter on examples of their relationship to the family project of the colonial administration for purposes of brevity. Utilizing examples from other colonized elite communities might have taken this chapter's argument in slightly different directions. But the Straits Chinese community can be taken as somewhat representative of the colonizer-colonized elite relationship in a broad sense because, as Holden notes, "there is evidence that the kind of modern Asian subjectivity which came into being through the body project of [the Straits Chinese elites] . . . moved beyond the confines of a Straits Chinese community to a larger Anglophone elite" (1999, 73).

20. For an analysis of the gendered dimensions of the reform movement, in particular, see Doran (1997).

21. Again, the phrase "tensions of empire" alludes to Cooper and Stoler (1997). See note 4.

22. Khoo Hooi Leong v. Khoo Chong Yeok (1930, 127–128).

23. Khoo Hooi Leong v. Khoo Chong Yeok (1930, 128).

24. National Archives of Singapore, HB 778/47/III, HDB Press Statement, August 4, 1967.

25. Two rare analyses that see the colonial beginnings of Singapore's housing program as consequential are Clancey (2003) and Loh (2007).

26. The report did not contain complete uniformity on this point. A. W. Still, the editor of the *Straits Times*, was a lone voice calling for the encouragement of marriage and the provision of single-family dwellings as a counter to "social evils" (Singapore 1918, C107).

27. National Archives of Singapore, HB 778/47/2, Singapore Improvement Trust Housing Register Information Quiz.

28. National Archives of Singapore, HB 778/47/2, J. C. Lee, Estates Manager, "Authorised Occupation of Trust Flats," appendix A.

29. National Archives of Singapore, HB 778/47/2, J. C. Lee, Estates Manager.

30. Housing Development Board, "Thinking of Buying a HDB Flat," *Our Home* (1972a, 3). Today, unmarried, divorced, or widowed individuals and single parents become eligible to buy HDB flats after age thirty-five. But even then they are eligible to purchase only resale, rather than new, flats and they are granted a much smaller subsidy than family

applicants receive. See www.hdb.gov.sg for full statements of eligibility criteria for various flat ownership and sublet schemes.

31. See also Kaye (1960).

Chapter 4. Making the Modern Model Family at Home

1. For instance, the 1921 census report states, "The value of statistics as to marriage in a country like British Malaya is not very great. . . . As a proof of the accuracy of this statement, it may be mentioned that, while in England and Wales in 1911 there were 1,021 married women to 1,000 married men, in British Malaya in 1921 the ratio was only 788 to 1,000; that is, nearly one married man in four had left his wife in another country" (Nathan 1922).

2. The five Shared Values were established in 1991 as a national ideology intended to maintain social cohesion as Singapore society evolved. They are nation before community and society above self, family as the basic unit of society, community support and respect for the individual, consensus not conflict, and racial and religious harmony (see Parliament of Singapore 1991).

3. Thus PM Lee mentioned HDB to support his description of the city-state as a "straight" space in his 2007 speech to Parliament rejecting calls to repeal Section 377A of the Penal Code. Recall his statement that "the overall society . . . remains conventional, it remains straight. . . . The family is the basic building block of our society. It has been so and, by policy, we have reinforced this and we want to keep it so. . . . If we look at the way our Housing and Development Board [HDB] flats are, our neighbourhoods, our new towns, they are, by and large, the way Singaporeans live" (Lee 2007).

4. See chapter 3, note 30 for details of HDB eligibility criteria.

5. I examined an almost complete set of the magazine in the holdings of the National University of Singapore's Singapore and Malaysia Collection. I went through the contents of each issue and systematically noted the subject area of each article and editorial. Articles related to family matters (including regular columns on family size, early childhood education, nutrition, and pregnancy and birth as well as a range of articles on various topics) are particularly concentrated in the 1972 to 1979 issues of the magazine. This is not surprising given the predominant antinatalist policy focus that persisted until 1980 in Singapore as well as the fact that demographic change in terms of household composition was most dramatic in the 1970s.

6. Advice on home decoration is the focus of Jacobs and Cairns's analysis. They show "how the cultivation of the interior became central to the 'covenant' between people and state" (2008, 592).

7. "Happy Families," *Our Home* (Housing Development Board 1976b, 28).

8. "The Guidance Clinic," *Our Home* (Housing Development Board 1976a, 4).

9. "'I Do'—the Later the Better," *Our Home* (Housing Development Board 1979, 2).

10. "What Family Planning Can Do," *Our Home* (Housing Development Board 1972b, 23).

11. This practice is mentioned in the Singapore Family Planning and Population Board annual reports from 1966 to 1972.

12. For an account of the clash between activists and the PAP on this issue and its importance in the history of the Singapore feminist movement, see Lyons (2004b).

13. On experiences of "singlehood" as a conjuncture of state, community, and family norms, see Ramdas (2012).

14. See National Population and Talent Division, *A Sustainable Population for a Dynamic Singapore: Population White Paper* (2013). The National Population and Talent Division is a ministry in the Prime Minister's Office with the following responsibilities: population augmentation; supporting marriage and parenthood; talent attraction and retention; immigration, naturalization, and integration of newcomers; and engaging overseas Singaporeans. See http://population.sg/whitepaper/resource-files/population-white -paper.pdf.

15. On this point, see Loh (2010).

16. For instance, see Chua (1997), Hassan (1977), and Salaff (1988).

17. See also Jose and Doran (1997) and Yeoh and Willis (2005).

18. For a discussion of Singapore's falling fertility rate, see Teo (2011, 25–26 and 48–50).

19. While the dominant discourse of the government-run mainstream press touts the necessity of these policies, worries over employment prospects for nonimmigrant Singaporeans and over the nature of Singaporean identity in this new cosmopolis are well articulated in the independent online press. For a full examination of the adoption of these new policies to encourage "foreign talent" to become Singapore citizens and the social tensions that have arisen as a result, which are beyond the scope of this chapter, see Nasir and Turner (2014).

20. From 2.9 percent of the population in 1970 (Yeoh 2006), the total share of the nonresident population rose to approximately 5 percent in 1980, 10 percent in 1990, and 19 percent in 2000. In absolute terms, the nonresident population was 131,820 in 1980, 331,264 in 1990, and 754,524 in 2000. See Teo and Piper (2009).

21. See https://www.ica.gov.sg/news_details.aspx?nid=2913.

22. For additional explicit statements of the government's "talent-centric" approach, see the website of the National Population and Talent Division (https://www.nptd.gov .sg) and Economic Strategies Committee (2010).

23. For a discussion of the intimate lives of migrant workers in Singapore, see Kitiarsa (2008). For analyses of the relationship between sexuality and migration in a range of contexts, also see Mai and King (2009) and Walsh, Shen, and Willis (2008).

24. See Yeoh (2006) for a discussion of the labor policies that shape Singapore's drive to maintain global city status. The recruitment of highly skilled "foreign talent" who can relatively easily attain permanent resident status and citizenship stands in stark contrast to a raft of policies that ensure that unskilled "foreign workers" remain transient and can be easily repatriated. As Yeoh notes, "Work permit holders enjoy few privileges and face restrictions such as the non-eligibility for the dependent's pass allowing them to bring their spouses and children with them. . . . They are only allowed to work for the employer and in the occupation as reflected in the work permit and cannot therefore gain access to the local labour market. In addition, they may not marry Singaporeans, and are subject to regular medical examination" (2006, 30). The "foreign workers" category contains workers employed almost exclusively in two fields, construction and domestic work. While construction workers are expressly prohibited from HDB rental or ownership, domestic workers are also similarly excluded. This group of workers is not specifically mentioned in HDB's tenancy regulations because they are required to live in their employer's home.

25. Available at http://www.straitstimes.com/ST%2BForum/Online%2BStory/STIStory
_277226.html.

Epilogue. From Queer to Decolonized

1. Promotional video, "Come Make Pink Dot: 18 June 2011," www.pinkdotsg.blogspot.

2. "It's Home for Now" (*Straits Times* 2009b).

3. Pink Dot 2012 campaign video, http://pinkdot.sg/someday-directors-note-2/.

4. See a rebuttal by Laleh Khalili, "In Search of the 'Merits' of Colonialism," *Al Jazeera*,
January 15, 2018, http://www.aljazeera.com/indepth/opinion/search-merits-colonialism
-180114143810705.html.

BIBLIOGRAPHY

Abraham, J. 2009. *Metropolitan Lovers: The Homosexuality of Cities*. University of Minnesota Press, Minneapolis.

Andersson, J. 2015. "Wilding" in the West Village: Queer space, racism, and Jane Jacobs hagiography. *International Journal of Urban and Regional Research* 39(2): 265–283.

Andersson, J. 2011. Vauxhall's post-industrial pleasure gardens: "Death wish" and hedonism in 21st-century London. *Urban Studies* 48(1): 85–100.

Ang, I., and J. Stratton. 1995. The Singapore way of multiculturalism: Western concepts / Asian cultures. *Sojourn: Journal of Social Issues in Southeast Asia* 10(1): 65–89.

Arondekar, A. 2005. Without a trace: Sexuality and the colonial archive. *Journal of the History of Sexuality* 14(1–2): 10–27.

Asher, M. G., and A. Nandy. 2008. Singapore's policy responses to ageing, inequality and poverty: An assessment. *International Social Security Review* 61(1): 41–60.

Bacchetta, P., F. El-Tayeb, and J. Haritaworn. 2015. Queer of colour formations and translocal spaces in Europe. *Environment and Planning D: Society and Space* 33(5): 769–778.

Baey, G. 2010. *Borders and the Exclusion of Migrant Bodies in Singapore's Global City-State*. MA thesis, Department of Geography, Queens University, Kingston, Canada.

Bailey, M. 2013. *Butch Queens up in Pumps: Gender, Performance, and Ballroom Culture in Detroit*. University of Michigan Press, Ann Arbor.

Barr, M. 2003. Perpetual revisionism in Singapore: The limits of change. *Pacific Review* 16(1): 77–97.

Barr, M. D., and J. Low. 2005. Assimilation as multiracialism: The case of Singapore's Malays. *Asian Ethnicity* 6(3): 161–182.

Barr, M. D., and C. A. Trocki (eds.). 2009. *Paths Not Taken: Political Pluralism in Postwar Singapore*. National University of Singapore Press, Singapore.

Bell, D., and J. Binnie. 2004. Authenticating queer space: Citizenship, urbanism and governance. *Urban Studies* 41(9): 1807–1820.

Bell, D., and G. Valentine. 1995. Introduction: Orientations. In D. Bell and G. Valentine (eds.). *Mapping Desire: Geographies of Sexualities*. Routledge, London, 1–27.

Benedicto, B. 2014. *Under Bright Lights: Gay Manila and the Global Scene*. University of Minnesota Press, Minneapolis.

Benjamin, G. 1976. The cultural logic of Singapore's "multiracialism." In R. Hassan (ed.). *Singapore: Society in Transition*. Oxford University Press, Kuala Lumpur, 115–133.

Berlant, L. 1998. Intimacy: A special issue. *Critical Inquiry* 24(2): 281–288.

Berlant, L., and M. Warner. 1998. Sex in public. *Critical Inquiry* 24(2):547–566.

Binnie, J. 2014. Relational comparison, queer urbanism and worlding cities. *Geography Compass* 8(8): 590–599.

Bleys, R. 1995. *The Geography of Perversion: Male-to-Male Sexual Behavior Outside the West and the Ethnographic Imagination, 1750–1918*. New York University Press, New York.

Braddell, S. R. 1934. *The Lights of Singapore*. Methuen, London.

Brenner, N. 2013. Theses on urbanization. *Public Culture* 25(1): 85–114.

Brenner, N. 1998. Global cities, "glocal" states: Global city formation and state territorial restructuring in contemporary Europe. *Review of International Political Economy* 5(1): 1–37.

Briggs, L. 2002. *Reproducing Empire: Race, Sex, Science, and U.S. Imperialism in Puerto Rico*. University of California Press, Berkeley.

Brown, G. 2008. Urban (homo)sexualities: Ordinary cities and ordinary sexualities. *Geography Compass* 2(4): 1215–1231.

Brown, W. 2008. *Regulating Aversion: Tolerance in the Age of Identity and Empire*. Princeton University Press, Princeton, N.J.

Bunnell, T. 2015. Antecedent cities and inter-referencing effects: Learning from and extending beyond critiques of neoliberalism. *Urban Studies* 52(11): 1983–2000.

Bunnell, T. 1999. Views from above and below: The Petronas Twin Towers and/in contesting visions of development in contemporary Malaysia. *Singapore Journal of Tropical Geography* 20(1): 1–23.

Butler, J. 1999. *Gender Trouble: Feminism and the Subversion of Identity*. Routledge, New York.

Butler, J. 1994. Against proper objects. *differences* 6(2–3): 1–26.

Carter, J. B. 2005. Theory, methods, praxis: The history of sexuality and the question of evidence. *Journal of the History of Sexuality* 14(1/2): 1–9.

Chang, T. C. 2000. Renaissance revisited: Singapore as a global city for the arts. *International Journal of Urban and Regional Research* 24(4): 818–831.

Chang, T. C., and S. Huang. 2011. Reclaiming the city: Waterfront development in Singapore. *Urban Studies* 48(10): 2085–2100.

Chang, T. C., S. Huang, and V. R. Savage. 2004. On the waterfront: Globalization and urbanization in Singapore. *Urban Geography* 25(5): 413–436.

Chauncey, G. 1994. *Gay New York: Gender, Urban Culture and the Making of the Gay Male World 1890–1940*. Basic Books, New York.

Cheah, B. 2007. Deconstructing the majority. *The Online Citizen*, October 24. http://theonlinecitizen.com/2007/10/24/deconstructing-the-majority/.

Cheng, Y. 2015. Biopolitical geographies of student life: Private higher education and citizenship life-making in Singapore. *Annals of the Association of American Geographers* 105(5): 1078–1093.

Chisholm, D. 2004. *Queer Constellations: Subcultural Space in the Wake of the City*. University of Minnesota Press, Minneapolis.

Chong, T (ed.). 2013. *The Aware Saga: Civil Society and Public Morality in Singapore*. National University of Singapore Press, Singapore.

Chua, B. H. 2011. Singapore as model: Planning innovations, knowledge experts. In A. Roy and A. Ong (eds.). *Worlding Cities: Asian Experiments and the Art of Being Global*. Wiley-Blackwell, Malden, Mass., 29–54.

Chua, B. H. 2010. The cultural logic of a capitalist single-party state, Singapore. *Postcolonial Studies* 13(4): 335–350.

Chua, B. H. 2008. Foreword. In H. Lysa and J. Huang (eds.). *The Scripting of a National History: Singapore and Its Pasts.* National University of Singapore Press, Singapore, ix–xi.

Chua, B. H. 1997. *Political Legitimacy and Housing: Stakeholding in Singapore.* Routledge, New York.

Chua, B. H. 1995. *Communitarian Ideology and Democracy in Singapore.* Routledge, London.

Chua, L. 2015. *Mobilizing Gay Singapore: Rights and Resistance in an Authoritarian State.* Temple University Press, Philadelphia.

Chua, L. 2012. Pragmatic resistance, law, and social movements in authoritarian states: The case of gay collective action in Singapore. *Law and Society Review* 46(4): 713–748.

Chua, L. 2003. Saying no: Sections 377 and 377A of the Penal Code. *Singapore Journal of Legal Studies* 2003: 209–261.

Clancey, G. 2003. Toward a spatial history of emergency: Notes from Singapore. Asia Research Institute Working Paper Series no. 8. National University of Singapore, Singapore.

Cohen, C. 1997. Punks, bulldaggers, and welfare queens: The radical potential of queer politics? *GLQ* 3(4): 437–465.

Comaroff, J. 2007. Ghostly topographies: Landscapes and biopower in modern Singapore. *Cultural Geographies* 14(1): 56–73.

Cooper, F., and A. L. Stoler (eds.). 1997. *Tensions of Empire: Colonial Cultures in a Bourgeois World.* University of California Press, Berkeley.

Delaney, S. 1999. *Times Square Red, Times Square Blue.* New York University Press, New York.

D'Emilio, J. 1983. Capitalism and gay identity. In A. Snitow, C. Stansell, and S. Thompson (eds.). *Powers of Desire: The Politics of Sexuality.* Monthly Review Press, New York, 100–113.

Derickson, K. D. 2015. Urban geography I: Locating urban theory in the "urban age." *Progress in Human Geography* 39(5): 647–657.

Devan, J. 2007. 377A debate and the rewriting of pluralism. *Straits Times*, October 27.

Doan, P. 2007. Queers in the American city: Transgendered perceptions of urban space. *Gender, Place & Culture* 14(1): 57–74.

Doran, C. 1997. The Chinese cultural reform movement in Singapore: Singaporean Chinese identities and reconstructions of gender. *Sojourn* 12(1): 92–107.

Doshi, T., and P. Coclanis. 1999. The economic architect: Goh Keng Swee. In P. R. Lam and K. Y. L. Tan (eds.). *Lee's Lieutenants: Singapore's Old Guard.* Allen & Unwin, St. Leonard's, NSW, 24–43.

Drakakis-Smith, D., E. Graham, P. Teo, and G. L. Ooi. 1993. Singapore: Reversing the demographic transition to meet labour needs. *Scottish Geographical Magazine* 109(3): 152–163.

Driskill, Q.-L., C. Finley, B. J. Gilley. and S. Morgensen (eds.). 2011. *Queer Indigenous Studies: Critical Interventions in Theory, Politics and Literature.* University of Arizona Press, Tucson.

Duggan, L. 2003. *The Twilight of Equality? Neoliberalism, Cultural Politics and the Attack on Democracy*. Beacon, Boston.

Economic Strategies Committee. 2010. *Report of the Subcommittee on Making Singapore a Leading Global City*. Singapore. http://app.mof.gov.sg/data/cmsresource/ESC%20Report/Subcommittee%20on%20Making%20Singapore%20a%20Leading%20Global%20City.pdf.

Edelman, L. 2004. *No Future: Queer Theory and the Death Drive*. Duke University Press, Durham, N.C.

Elegant, S. 2003. The lion in winter. *Time Asia*, July 30.

Eng, D. L., with J. Halberstam and J. E. Muñoz. 2005. Introduction: What's queer about queer studies now? *Social Text* 23(3–4): 1–17.

Engebretsen, E. 2014. *Queer Women in Urban China*. Routledge, New York.

Ferguson, R. 2004. *Aberrations in Black: Toward a Queer of Color Critique*. University of Minnesota Press, Minneapolis.

Florida, R. 2017. *The New Urban Crisis: How Our Cities Are Increasing Inequality, Deepening Segregation, and Failing the Middle Class—and What We Can Do about It*. Basic Books, New York.

Florida, R. 2002. *The Rise of the Creative Class: And How It's Transforming Work, Leisure, Community and Everyday Life*. Basic Books, New York.

Foucault, M. 1978. *The History of Sexuality: An Introduction*. Vol. 1. Vintage, New York.

Freccero, C. 2007. Queer times. *South Atlantic Quarterly* 106(3): 485–494.

Friedmann, J. 1986. The world city hypothesis. *Development and Change* 17: 69–83.

George, C. 2017. *Singapore, Incomplete: Reflections on a First World Nation's Arrested Political Development*. Woodsville News, Singapore.

George, C. 2012. *Freedom from the Press: Journalism and State Power in Singapore*. National University of Singapore Press, Singapore.

George, C. 2000. *Singapore: The Air-Conditioned Nation: Essays on the Politics of Comfort and Control, 1990–2000*. Landmark Books, Singapore.

Ghertner, D. A. 2015. *Rule by Aesthetics: World-Class City Making in Delhi*. Oxford University Press, New York.

Goh, C. T. 2007. Making Singapore a global city. Speech at the Singapore Institute of Architects 46th Annual Dinner, Singapore, May 4.

Goh, C. T. 2003. From the valley to the highlands. National Day Rally speech, Singapore, August 17. http://www.nas.gov.sg/archivesonline/speeches/view-html?filename=2003081707.htm.

Goh, C. T. 2000. Building a multiracial nation through integration, Speech at the Second Convention of Singapore Malay/Muslim Professionals, 5 November. In *Speeches: A Bimonthly Selection of Ministerial Speeches (November–December)*. Ministry of Information and the Arts, Singapore, 13–21.

Goh, C. T. 1999. First-world economy, world-class home. National Day Rally speech, Singapore. http://www.nas.gov.sg/archivesonline/speeches/view-html?filename=1999082202.htm.

Goh, D. P. S. 2010. Unofficial contentions: The postcoloniality of Straits Chinese political discourse in the Straits Settlements Legislative Council. *Journal of Southeast Asian Studies* 41(3): 483–507.

Goh, D., M. Gabrielpillai, P. Holden, and G. C. Khoo (eds.). 2009. *Race and Multiculturalism in Malaysia and Singapore*. Routledge, London.

Goh, D., and P. Holden. 2009. Introduction: Postcoloniality, race and multiculturalism. In D. Goh, M. Gabrielpillai, P. Holden, and G. C. Khoo (eds.). *Race and Multiculturalism in Malaysia and Singapore*. Routledge, London, 1–16.

Goh, K. 2018. Safe cities and queer spaces: The urban politics of radical LGBT activism. *Annals of the American Association of Geographers* 108(2): 463–477.

Goh, K. S. 1972. Social, political and institutional aspects of development planning. In *The Economics of Modernization: The Essays and Speeches of Goh Keng Swee*. Asia Pacific Press, Singapore, 60–82.

Goh, R. B. H. 2005. *Contours of Culture: Space and Social Difference in Singapore*. Hong Kong University Press, Hong Kong.

Goh, R. B. H. 2001. Ideologies of "upgrading" in Singapore public housing: Post-modern style, globalization, and class construction in the built environment. *Urban Studies* 38(9): 1589–1604.

Gopinath, G. 2005. *Impossible Desires: Queer Diasporas and South Asian Public Cultures*. Duke University Press, Durham, N.C.

Grice, K., and D. Drakakis-Smith. 1985. The role of the state in shaping development: Two decades of growth in Singapore. *Transactions of the Institute of British Geographers* 10(3): 347–359.

Gugler, J. (ed.). 2004. *World Cities beyond the West: Globalization, Development, and Inequality*. Cambridge University Press, New York.

Hall, P. 1966. *The World Cities*. Heinemann, London.

Halley, J. E. 2000. "Like race" arguments. In J. Butler, J. Guillory, and K. Thomas (eds.). *What's Left of Theory? New Works on the Politics of Literary Theory*. Routledge, New York, 40–74.

Hanhardt, C. 2013. *Safe Space: Gay Neighborhood History and the Politics of Violence*. Duke University Press, Durham, N.C.

Harper, T. N. 2001. Lim Chin Siong and the "Singapore Story." In J. Q. Tan and K. S. Jomo (eds.). *Comet in Our Sky: Lim Chin Siong in History*. INSAN, Kuala Lumpur, 3–55.

Harper, T. N. 1998. *The End of Empire and the Making of Malaya*. Cambridge University Press, Cambridge.

Harper, T. N. 1997. Globalism and the pursuit of authenticity: The making of a diasporic public sphere in Singapore. *Sojourn: Journal of Social Issues in Southeast Asia* 12(2): 261–292.

Hassan, R. 1977. *Families and Flats: A Study of Low Income Families in Public Housing*. Singapore University Press, Singapore.

Heng, G., and J. Devan. 1995. State fatherhood: The politics of nationalism, sexuality, and race in Singapore. In A. Ong and M. Peletz (eds.). *Bewitching Women, Pious Men: Gender and Body Politics in Southeast Asia*. University of California Press, Berkeley, 195–215.

Heng, R. 2001. Tiptoe out of the closet: The before and after of the increasingly visible gay community in Singapore. *Journal of Homosexuality* 40(3–4): 81–96.

Hirschman, C. 1986. The making of race in colonial Malaya: Political economy and racial ideology. *Sociological Forum* 1(2): 330–361.

Ho, E. L.-E. 2011. Migration trajectories of "highly skilled" middling transnationals: Singaporean transmigrants in London. *Population, Space and Place* 17(1): 116–129.

Ho, E. L.-E. 2009. Constituting citizenship through the emotions: Singaporean transmigrants in London. *Annals of the Association of American Geographers* 99(4): 788–804.

Ho, E. L.-E. 2006. Negotiating belonging and perceptions of citizenship in a transnational world: Singapore, a cosmopolis? *Social and Cultural Geography* 7(3): 385–401.

Ho, E. L.-E., and M. Boyle. 2015. Migration as development repackaged: The globalizing imperative of the Singaporean state's diaspora strategies. *Singapore Journal of Tropical Geography* 36(2): 164–182.

Ho, L.-C. 2012. Sorting citizens: Differentiated citizenship education in Singapore. *Journal of Curriculum Studies* 44(3): 403–428.

Holden, P. 2008. Postcolonial desire: Placing Singapore. *Postcolonial Studies* 28(3): 345–361.

Holden, P. 2003. Rethinking colonial discourse analysis and queer studies. In P. Holden and R. J. Ruppel (eds.). *Imperial Desire: Dissident Sexualities and Colonial Literature*. University of Minnesota Press, Minneapolis, 295–321.

Holden, P. 1999. The beginnings of "Asian modernity" in Singapore: A Straits Chinese body project. *Communal/Plural* 7(1): 59–78.

Houlbrook, M. 2005. *Queer London: Perils and Pleasures in the Sexual Metropolis, 1918–1957*. University of Chicago Press, Chicago.

Howell, P. 2009. *Geographies of Regulation: Policing Prostitution in Nineteenth-Century Britain and the Empire*. Cambridge University Press, New York.

Howell, P. 2004. Race, space and the regulation of prostitution in colonial Hong Kong. *Urban History* 31(2): 229–248.

Howell, P. 2000. Prostitution and racialised sexuality: The regulation of prostitution in Britain and the British Empire before the Contagious Diseases Act. *Environment and Planning D: Society and Space* 18(3): 321–339.

Hubbard, P. 2011. *Cities and Sexualities*. Routledge, New York.

Hubbard, P. 2008. Here, there, everywhere: The ubiquitous geographies of heteronormativity. *Geography Compass* 2(3): 640–658.

Hubbard, P. 2004. Cleansing the metropolis: Sex work and the politics of zero tolerance. *Urban Studies* 41(9): 1687–1702.

Huff, W. G. 1995. The developmental state, government, and Singapore's economic development since 1960. *World Development* 23(8): 1421–1438.

Jackson, P. 2011. *Queer Bangkok: 21st Century Markets, Media and Rights*. Hong Kong University Press, Hong Kong.

Jacobs, J. M., and S. S. Cairns. 2008. The modern touch: Interior design and modernization in post-independence Singapore. *Environment and Planning A* 40(3): 572–595.

Jacobs, J. M., and R. Fincher. 1998. Introduction. In R. Fincher and J. M. Jacobs (eds.). *Cities of Difference*. Guilford, New York, 1–25.

Jagose, A. 1996. *Queer Theory: An Introduction*. New York University Press, New York.

Jones, G. 2012. Late marriage and low fertility in Singapore: The limits of policy. *Japanese Journal of Population* 10(1): 89–101.

Jose, J., and C. Doran. 1997. Marriage and marginalization in Singaporean politics. *Journal of Contemporary Asia* 27(4): 475–488.

Kanai, J. M. 2015. Buenos Aires beyond (homo)sexualized urban entrepreneurialism: The geographies of queered tango. *Antipode* 47(3): 652–670.

Kanna, A. 2011. *Dubai, the City as Corporation*. University of Minnesota Press, Minneapolis.

Keil, R., G. Wekerle, and D. V. J. Bell (eds.). 1996. *Local Places in the Age of the Global City*. Black Rose Books, Montreal.

King, A. 1991. *Urbanism, Colonialism and the World Economy: Cultural and Spatial Foundations of the World Urban System*. Routledge, New York.

King, R., and D. E. Idawati. 2010. Surabaya kampung and distorted communication. *Sojourn: Journal of Social Issues in Southeast Asia* 25(2): 213–233.

Kitiarsa, P. 2008. Thai migrants in Singapore: State, intimacy and desire. *Gender, Place & Culture* 15(6): 595–610.

Kong, L. 2000. Cultural policy in Singapore: Negotiating economic and socio-cultural agendas. *Geoforum* 31(4): 409–424.

Krätke, S. 2011. *The Creative Capital of Cities: Interactive Knowledge Creation and the Urbanization Economies of Innovation*. Wiley-Blackwell, Malden, Mass.

Kuo, E. C. Y., and A. K. Wong. 1979. Some observations on the study. In E. C. Y. Kuo and A. K. Wong (eds.). *The Contemporary Family in Singapore: Structure and Change*. Singapore University Press, Singapore, 3–16.

Kwok, K. W. 1999. The social architect: Goh Keng Swee. In P. R. Lam and K. Y. L. Tan (eds.). *Lee's Lieutenants: Singapore's Old Guard*. Allen & Unwin, St. Leonard's, NSW, 45–69.

Lam, P. R., and K. Y. L. Tan (eds.). 1999. *Lee's Lieutenants: Singapore's Old Guard*. Allen & Unwin, St. Leonard's, NSW.

Lee, H. L. 2007. Speech to Parliament on reading of Penal Code (Amendment) Bill, October 22, Singapore. http://sprs.parl.gov.sg/search/topic.jsp?currentTopicID=00002031-WA&currentPubID=00004748-WA&topicKey=00004748-WA.00002031-WA_1%2B%2B.

Lee, H. L. 2006. National Day Rally speech, August 20. http://www.nas.gov.sg/archivesonline/speeches/record-details/7e69abe9-115d-11e3-83d5-0050568939ad.

Lee, H. L. 2005. National Day Rally speech, August 21. http://www.nas.gov.sg/archivesonline/speeches/view-html?filename=2005082102.htm.

Lee, K. Y. 2000. *From Third World to First: The Singapore Story, 1965–2000*. HarperCollins, New York.

Lee, K. Y. 1966. National Day Rally speech, National Theatre of Singapore, Singapore, August 8.

Lee, Y.-S., and E.-J. Hwang. 2012. Global urban frontiers through policy transfer? Unpacking Seoul's creative city programmes. *Urban Studies* 49(13): 2817–2838.

Leifer, M. 2000. *Singapore's Foreign Policy: Coping with Vulnerability*. Routledge, London.

Leong, L. W.-T. 1995. Walking the tightrope: The role of action for AIDS in the provision of social services in Singapore. In G. Sullivan and L. W.-T. Leong (eds.). *Gays and Lesbians in Asia and the Pacific: Social and Human Services*. Harrington Park Press, Binghamton, N.Y., 11–30.

Levine, P. 1999. Modernity, medicine and colonialism: The contagious diseases ordinances in Hong Kong and the Straits Settlements. In A. Burton (ed.). *Gender, Sexuality and Colonial Modernities*. Routledge, London, 35–48.

Li, T. 1989. *Malays in Singapore: Culture, economy, and ideology*. Oxford University Press, Singapore.

Lim, E.-B. 2009. Performing the global university. *Social Text,* 27(4): 25–44.

Lim, E.-B. 2005a. Glocalqueering in New Asia: The politics of performing gay in Singapore. *Theatre Journal* 57(3): 383–405.

Lim, E.-B. 2005b. The Mardi Gras Boys of Singapore's English-language theatre. *Asian Theatre Journal* 22(2): 293–309.

Lim, K. C. 1989. Post-independence population planning and social development in Singapore. *GeoJournal* 18 (2): 163–174.

Lim, K. F. 2004. Where loves dares (not) speak its name: Homosexuality in Singapore. *Urban Studies* 41(9): 1759–1788.

Liow, E. 2011. The neoliberal-developmental state: Singapore as case study. *Critical Sociology* 38(2): 241–264.

Livermon, X. 2012. Queer(y)ing freedom: Black queer visibilities in postapartheid South Africa. *GLQ* 18(2–3): 297–323.

Lo, J., and G. Q. Huang (eds.). 2003. *People Like Us: Sexual Minorities in Singapore.* Select Books, Singapore.

Loh, K. S. 2013. *Squatters into Citizens: The 1961 Bukit Ho Swee Fire and the Making of Modern Singapore.* National University of Singapore Press, Singapore.

Loh, K. S. 2010. Dangerous migrants and the informal mobile city of post-war Singapore. *Mobilities* 5(2): 197–218.

Loh, K. S. 2009. Conflict and change at the margins: Emergency kampong clearance and the making of modern Singapore. *Asian Studies Review* 33(2): 139–159.

Loh, K. S. 2007. Black areas: Urban kampongs and power relations in post-war Singapore historiography. *Sojourn* 22(1): 1–29.

Loos, T. 2008. A history of sex and the state in Southeast Asia: Class, intimacy and invisibility. *Citizenship Studies* 12(1): 27–43.

Low, L. 2001. The Singapore developmental state in the new economy and polity. *Pacific Review* 14(3): 411–441.

Luckman, S., C. Gibson, and T. Lea. 2009. Mosquitoes in the mix: How transferable is creative city thinking? *Singapore Journal of Tropical Geography* 30(1): 70–85.

Luger, J. 2016. Singaporean "spaces of hope?": Activist geographies in the city-state. *City* 20(2): 186–203.

Luibhéid, E. 2013. *Pregnant on Arrival: Making the Illegal Immigrant.* University of Minnesota Press, Minneapolis.

Lyons, L. 2004a. Sexing the nation: Normative heterosexuality and the construction of the "good" Singaporean citizen. In A. Branach-Kallas and K. Wieckowska (eds.). *The Nation of the Other: Constructions of Nation in Contemporary Cultural and Literary Discourses.* Nicholas Copernicus University Press, Torun, Poland, 79–96.

Lyons, L. 2004b. *A State of Ambivalence: The Feminist Movement in Singapore.* Brill, Leiden.

Mai, N., and R. King (eds.). 2009. Love, sexuality and migration. Special issue of *Mobilities* 4(3).

Manalansan, M. 2015. Queer worldings: The messy art of being global in Manila and New York. *Antipode* 43(3): 566–579.

Manalansan, M. 2005. Race, violence, and neoliberal spatial politics in the global city. *Social Text* 23: 141–155.

Manalansan, M. 2003. *Global Divas: Filipino Gay Men in the Diaspora.* Duke University Press, Durham, N.C.

Manderson, L. 1997. Colonial desires: Sexuality, race, and gender in British Malaya. *Journal of the History of Sexuality* 7(3): 372–388.

Manderson, L. 1996. *Sickness and the State: Health and Illness in Colonial Malaya, 1870–1940.* Cambridge University Press, New York.

Markusen, A. 2006. Urban development and the politics of a creative class: Evidence from a study of artists. *Environment and Planning A* 38(10): 1921–1940.

Martin, F. 2003. *Situating Sexualities: Queer Representation in Taiwanese Fiction, Film and Public Culture.* Hong Kong University Press, Hong Kong.

McCann, E. 2004. Urban political economy beyond the "global city." *Urban Studies* 41(12): 2315–2333.

McCann, E., A. Roy, and K. Ward. 2013. Urban pulse—assembling/worlding cities. *Urban Geography* 34(5): 581–589.

McClintock, A. 1995. *Imperial Leather: Race, Gender and Sexuality in the Colonial Contest.* Routledge, New York.

McFarlane, C. 2008. Urban shadows: Materiality, the "southern city" and urban theory. *Geography Compass* 2(2): 340–358.

Merabet, S. 2014. *Queer Beirut.* University of Texas Press, Austin.

Misgav, C., and L. Johnston. 2014. Dirty dancing: The (non)fluid embodied geographies of a queer nightclub in Tel Aviv. *Social and Cultural Geography* 15(7): 730–746.

Montsion, J. M. 2012. When talent meets mobility: Un/desirability in Singapore's new citizenship project. *Citizenship Studies* 16(3–4): 469–482.

Moser, S. 2012. Globalization and the construction of identity in two new Southeast Asian capitals: Putrajaya and Dompak. In X. Chen and A. Kanna (eds.). *Rethinking Global Urbanism: Comparative Insights from Secondary Cities.* Routledge, London, 169–189.

Moussawi, G. 2018. Queer exceptionalism and exclusion: Cosmopolitanism and inequalities in "gay-friendly" Beirut. *Sociological Review* 66(1): 174–190.

Muñoz, J. E. 2009. *Cruising Utopia: The Then and There of Queer Futurity.* New York University Press, New York.

Muñoz, J. E. 1999. *Disidentifications: Queers of Color and the Performance of Politics.* University of Minnesota Press, Minneapolis.

Muzaini, H., and B. Yeoh. 2007. Memory-making "from below": Rescaling remembrance at the Kranji War Memorial and Cemetery, Singapore. *Environment and Planning A* 39(6): 1288–1305.

Nasir, K. M., and B. S. Turner. 2014. *The Future of Singapore: Population, Society and the Nature of the State.* Routledge, London.

Nasir, K. M., and B. S. Turner. 2013. Governing as gardening: Reflections on soft authoritarianism in Singapore. *Citizenship Studies* 17(3–4): 339–352.

National Population and Talent Division. 2013. *A Sustainable Population for a Dynamic Singapore: Population White Paper.* http://population.sg/whitepaper/resource-files/population-white-paper.pdf.

Neo, H. 2007. Challenging the developmental state: Nature conservation in Singapore. *Asia Pacific Viewpoint* 48(2): 186–199.

Olds, K. 2012. Deterritorializing academic freedom: Reflections inspired by Yale-NUS College (and the London Eye). *Inside Higher Ed.* https://www.insidehighered.com/blogs/globalhighered/deterritorializing-academic-freedom-reflections-inspired-yale-nus-college-and.

Olds, K. 2007. Global assemblage: Singapore, foreign universities and the construction of a "global education hub." *World Development* 35(6): 959–975.

Olds, K., and H. Yeung. 2004. Pathways to global city formation: A view from the developmental city-state of Singapore. *Review of International Political Economy* 11(3): 489–521.

Ong, A., and A. Roy (eds.). 2011. *Worlding Cities: Asian Experiments and the Art of Being Global.* University of Minnesota Press, Minneapolis.

Oswin, N. (ed.). 2015. World, city, queer. Theme issue of *Antipode* 47(3).

Oswin, N. 2008. Critical geographies and the uses of sexuality: Deconstructing queer space. *Progress in Human Geography* 32(1): 89–103.

Papayanis, M. A. 2000. Sex and the revanchist city: Zoning out pornography in New York. *Environment and Planning D: Society and Space* 18(3): 341–353.

Parliament of Singapore. 1991. White paper on shared values. http://eresources.nlb.gov .sg/infopedia/articles/SIP_542_2004-12-18.html.

Peck, J. 2005. Struggling with the creative class. *International Journal of Urban and Regional Research* 29(4): 740–790.

Perry, M., L. Kong, and B. Yeoh. 1997. *Singapore: A Developmental City State.* Wiley, London.

Peterson, W. 2001. *Theater and the Politics of Culture in Contemporary Singapore.* Wesleyan University Press, Middleton, Conn.

Phillips, R. 2006. *Sex, Politics and Empire: A Postcolonial Geography.* Manchester University Press, Manchester.

Pitman, B. 2002. Re-mediating the spaces of reality television: *America's Most Wanted* and the case of Vancouver's missing women. *Environment and Planning A* 34(1): 167–184.

Poon, A. 2009. Pick and mix for a global city: Race and cosmopolitanism in Singapore. In D. Goh, M. Gabrielpillai, P. Holden, and G. C. Khoo (eds.). *Race and Multiculturalism in Malaysia and Singapore.* Routledge, London, 70–85.

Povinelli, E. 2006. *The Empire of Love: Toward a Theory of Intimacy, Genealogy, and Carnality.* Duke University Press, Durham, N.C.

Pow, C.-P. 2014. License to travel: Policy assemblage and the "Singapore model." *City* 18(3): 287–386.

Pow, C.-P. 2013. Consuming private security: Consumer citizenship and defensive urbanism in Singapore. *Theoretical Criminology* 17(2): 179–196.

Pow, C.-P. 2011. Living it up: Super-rich enclave and transnational elite urbanism in Singapore. *Geoforum* 42(3): 382–393.

Pow, C.-P. 2002. Urban entrepreneurialism and downtown transformation in Marina Centre, Singapore: A case study of Suntec City. In T. Bunnell, L. B. W. Drummond, and K. C. Ho (eds.). *Critical Reflections on Cities in Southeast Asia.* Times Academic Press, Singapore, 153–184.

Puar, J. 2007. *Terrorist Assemblages: Homonationalism in Queer Times.* Duke University Press, Durham, N.C.

Puar, J. 2002. A transnational feminist critique of queer tourism. *Antipode* 34(5): 935–946.

Purcell, V. 1965. *The Memoirs of a Malayan Official.* Cassell, London.

Raimondo, M. 2005. "AIDS capital of the world": Representing race, sex and space in Belle Glade, Florida. *Gender, Place & Culture* 12(1): 53–70.

Rajaratnam, S. [1972] 1977. Singapore: The global city. In T.-B. Wee (ed.). *The Future of Singapore: The Global City*. University Education Press, Singapore.

Ramdas, K. 2012. Women in waiting? Singlehood, marriage and family in Singapore. *Environment and Planning A* 44(4): 832–848.

Reddy, C. 2005. Asian diasporas, neoliberalism, and family: Reviewing the case for homosexual asylum in the context of family rights. *Social Text* 23(3–4): 101–119.

Robinson, J. 2016. Thinking cities through elsewhere: Comparative tactics for a more global urban studies. *Progress in Human Geography* 40(1): 3–29.

Robinson, J. 2014. New geographies of theorizing the urban: Putting comparison to work for global urban studies. In S. Parnell and S. Oldfield (eds.). *The Routledge Handbook on Cities of the Global South*. Routledge, New York, 57–70.

Robinson, J. 2006. *Ordinary Cities: Between Modernity and Development*. Routledge, London.

Robinson, J. 2002. Global and world cities: A view from off the map. *International Journal of Urban and Regional Research* 26(3): 531–554.

Rofel, L. 2007. *Desiring China: Experiments in Neoliberalism, Sexuality and Public Culture*. Duke University Press, Durham, N.C.

Roy, A. 2014a. Slumdog cities: Rethinking subaltern urbanism. *International Journal of Urban and Regional Research* 35(2): 223–238.

Roy, A. 2014b. Worlding the South: Toward a post-colonial urban theory. In S. Parnell and S. Oldfield (eds.). *The Routledge Handbook on Cities of the Global South*. Routledge, New York, 9–20.

Rushbrook, D. 2002. Cities, queer space, and the cosmopolitan tourist. *GLQ* 8(1–2): 183–206.

Salaff, J. W. 2004. Singapore: Forming the family for a world city. In J. Gugler (ed.). *World Cities beyond the West: Globalization, Development, and Inequality*. Cambridge University Press, New York, 240–267.

Salaff, J. W. 1988. *State and Family in Singapore: Restructuring a Developing Society*. Cornell University Press, Ithaca, N.Y.

Sassen, S. 1991. *The Global City: New York, London, Tokyo*. Princeton University Press, Princeton, N.J.

Seitz, D. 2015. The trouble with *Flag Wars*: Rethinking sexuality in critical urban theory. *International Journal of Urban and Regional Research* 39(2): 251–264.

Shah, N. 2012. *Stranger Intimacy: Contesting Race, Sexuality and the Law in the North American West*. University of California Press, Berkeley.

Shah, N. 2001. *Contagious Divides: Epidemics and Race in San Francisco's Chinatown*. University of California Press, Berkeley.

Shah, S. 2014. *Street Corner Secrets: Sex, Work and Migration in the City of Mumbai*. Duke University Press, Durham, N.C.

Shatkin, G. 2014. Reinterpreting the meaning of the "Singapore model": State capitalism and urban planning. *International Journal of Urban and Regional Research* 38(1): 116–137.

Simone, A. 2010. *City Life from Jakarta to Dakar: Movements at the Crossroads*. Routledge, London.

Sin, C. H. 2003. The politics of ethnic integration in Singapore: Malay "regrouping" as an ideological construct. *International Journal of Urban and Regional Research* 27(3): 527–544.

Singapore Family Planning and Population Board. 1968. *Family Planning: A Series of 12 Papers on Family Planning from Dec. 1965 to Dec. 1967*. Ministry of Health, Singapore.

Singapore Ministry of Home Affairs. 2006. Consultation paper on the proposed Penal Code amendments. www.agc.gov.sg/publications/docs/Penal_Code_Amendment _Bill_ Consultation_Paper.pdf.

Singapore Ministry of Manpower. 2009. Employment of Foreign Manpower Act (Chapter 91A). http://www.mom.gov.sg/Documents/services-forms/passes/WPSPass Conditions.pdf.

Singapore Ministry of Trade and Industry. 2003. *Report of the Economic Committee: New Challenges, Fresh Goals—Towards a Dynamic Global City*. https://www.mti.gov .sg/ResearchRoom/Documents/app.mti.gov.sg/data/pages/507/doc/ERC_Full_Report .pdf.

Singapore National Family Council and Ministry of Community Development, Youth and Sports. 2009. Foreword to *Family First: State of the Family Report 2009*. NFC Secretariat, Singapore. https://app.msf.gov.sg/Portals/0/Summary/research/NFCStateofthe FamilyReport2009.pdf.

Smith, A. 2010. Queer theory and native studies: The heteronormativity of settler colonialism. *GLQ* 16(1–2): 42–68.

Smith, M. P. 2001. *Transnational Urbanism: Locating Globalization*. Blackwell, Malden, Mass.

Snorton, C. R. 2017. *Black on Both Sides: A Racial History of Trans Identity*. University of Minnesota Press, Minneapolis.

Sparke, M., J. Sidaway, T. Bunnell, and C. Grundy-Warr. 2004. Triangulating the borderless world: Geographies of power in the Indonesia-Malaysia-Singapore Growth Triangle. *Transactions of the Institute of British Geographers* 29(4): 485–498.

Stoler, A. L. 2002. *Carnal Knowledge and Imperial Power: Race and the Intimate in Colonial Rule*. University of California Press, Berkeley.

Stoler, A. L. 1995. *Race and the Education of Desire: Foucault's History of Sexuality and the Colonial Order of Things*. Duke University Press, Durham, N.C.

Stout, N. 2015. *After Love: Queer Intimacy and Erotic Economies in Post-Soviet Cuba*. Duke University Press, Durham, N.C.

Straits Times. 2009a. Babies, women and foreigners. March 21.

Straits Times. 2009b. It's home for now. April 18.

Straits Times. 2004a. Panel backs idea of resort with casino. November 11.

Straits Times. 2004b. Singaporeans split evenly on casinos. September 25.

Straits Times. 2003a. It's not about gay rights—it's survival. July 9.

Straits Times. 2003b. Rebels—a prize catch. December 29.

Straits Times. 2002. Making room for the three T's. July 14.

Sun, S. H.-L. 2012. *Population Policy and Reproduction in Singapore: Making Future Citizens*. Routledge, New York.

Tan, C. 2012. "Our shared values" in Singapore: A Confucian perspective. *Educational Theory* 62(4): 449–463.

Tan, C. K. K. 2016. A "great affective divide": How gay Singaporeans overcome their double alienation. *Anthropological Forum* 26(1): 17–36.

Tan, C. K. K. 2009. "But they are like you and me": Gay civil servants and citizenship in a cosmopolitanizing Singapore. *City and Society* 21(1): 133–154.

Tan, K. P. 2007a. New politics for a renaissance city? In K. P. Tan (ed.). *Renaissance Singapore: Economy, Culture and Politics*. National University of Singapore Press, Singapore, 17–36.

Tan, K. P. (ed.). 2007b. *Renaissance Singapore? Economy, Culture and Politics*. National University of Singapore Press, Singapore.

Tan, K. P. 2003. Sexing up Singapore. *International Journal of Cultural Studies* 6(4): 402–423.

Tan, K. P., with G. L. J. Jin. 2007. Imagining the gay community in Singapore. *Critical Asian Studies* 39(2): 179–204.

Tang, D. T. S. 2011. *Conditional Spaces: Hong Kong Lesbian Desires and Everyday Life*. Hong Kong University Press, Hong Kong.

Teo, S. E., and L. Kong. 1997. Public housing in Singapore: Interpreting "quality" in the 1990s. *Urban Studies* 34(3): 441–452.

Teo, Y. Y. 2018. *This Is What Inequality Looks Like*. Ethos Books, Singapore.

Teo, Y. Y. 2016. Not everyone has "maids": Class differentials in the elusive quest for work-life balance. *Gender, Place & Culture* 23(8): 1164–1178.

Teo, Y. Y. 2011. *Neoliberal Morality in Singapore: How Family Policies Make State and Society*. Routledge, New York.

Teo, Y. Y. 2010. Shaping the Singapore family, producing the state and society. *Economy and Society* 39(3): 337–359.

Teo, Y. Y. 2007. Inequality for the greater good: Gendered state rule in Singapore. *Critical Asian Studies* 39(3): 423–445.

Teo, Y. Y., and N. Piper. 2009. Foreigners in our homes: Linking migration and family policies in Singapore. *Population, Space and Place* 15(1): 147–159.

Thoreson, R. R. 2014. *Transnational LGBT Activism: Working for Sexual Rights Worldwide*. University of Minnesota Press, Minneapolis.

Tongson, K. 2011. *Relocations: Queer Suburban Imaginaries*. New York University Press, New York.

Tremblay, M., D. Paternotte, and C. Johnson. 2011. *The Lesbian and Gay Movement and the State: Comparative Insights into a Transformed Relationship*. Ashgate, Surrey.

Tremewan, C. 1994. *The Political Economy of Social Control in Singapore*. St Martin's, London.

Trocki, C. A. 2006. *Singapore: Wealth, Power and the Culture of Control*. Routledge, New York.

Tucker, A. 2009. *Queer Visibilities: Space, Identity and Interaction in Cape Town*. Wiley-Blackwell, Malden, Mass.

UN-Habitat. 2012. *State of the World's Cities 2012–2013*. UN-Habitat, Nairobi.

United Nations. 2011. A/HRC/RES/17/19. Human rights, sexual orientation and gender identity. Resolution adopted by the Human Rights Council, July 14.

Valentine, G., and T. Skelton. 2003. Finding oneself, losing oneself: The lesbian and gay "scene" as a paradoxical space. *International Journal of Urban and Regional Research* 27(4): 849–866.

Vaughan, J. D. [1879] 1971. *The Manners and Customs of the Chinese of the Straits Settlements*. Oxford University Press, Singapore.

Waitt, G., and A. Gorman-Murray. 2011. Journeys and returns: Home, life narratives and remapping sexuality in a regional city. *International Journal of Urban and Regional Research* 35(6): 1239–1255.

Waldby, C. 2009. Singapore Biopolis: Bare life in the city-state. *East Asian Science, Technology and Society* 3: 367–383.

Walsh, K., H. H. Shen, and K. Willis (eds.). 2008. Heterosexuality and migration in Asia. Special issue of *Gender, Place & Culture* 15(6).

Wang, J. 2012. The developmental state in the global hegemony of neoliberalism: A new strategy for public housing in Singapore. *Geoforum* 29(6): 369–278.

Warner, M. 1995. Something queer about the nation-state. In C. Newfield and R. Strickland (eds.). *After Political Correctness: The Humanities and Society in the 1990s.* Westview, Boulder, Colo., 361–371.

Warner, M. 1993. Introduction. In M. Warner (ed.). *Fear of a Queer Planet: Queer Politics and Social Theory.* University of Minnesota Press, Minneapolis, vii–xxxi.

Warren, J. 2003. *Ah Ku and Karayuki-san: Prostitution in Singapore 1880–1940.* Singapore University Press, Singapore.

Watson, S. 2014. Spaces of difference: Challenging urban divisions from the north to the south. In S. Parnell and S. Oldfield (eds.). *The Routledge Handbook on Cities of the Global South.* Routledge, New York, 385–395.

Wee, C. J. W.-L. 2007. *The Asian Modern: Culture, Capitalist Development.* National University of Singapore Press, Singapore.

Wee, H. K., and J. Chia (eds.). 2016. *Singapore Dreaming: Managing Utopia.* Asian Urban Lab, Singapore.

Weiss, M. 2005. Who sets social policy in Metropolis? Economic positioning and social reform in Singapore. *New Political Science* 27(3): 267–289.

Winnubst, S. 2010. Review essay. No future: Queer theory and the death drive. *Environment and Planning D: Society and Space* 28(1): 178–183.

Wolch, J. 2003. Radical openness as method in urban geography. *Urban Geography* 24(8): 645–646.

Wong, A. K., and S. H. K. Yeh. 1985. *Housing a Nation: 25 Years of Public Housing in Singapore.* Housing Development Board, Singapore.

Wong, K. W., and T. Bunnell. 2006. "New economy" discourse and spaces in Singapore: A case study of One-North. *Environment and Planning A* 38(1): 69–83.

Wong, T., B. S. A. Yeoh, E. Graham, and P. Teo. 2004. Spaces of silence: Single parenthood and the "normal family" in Singapore. *Population, Space and Place* 10(1): 43–58.

Yao, S. 2007. *Singapore: The State and the Culture of Excess.* Routledge, New York.

Yao, S. 1999. Social virtues as cultural text: Colonial desire and the Chinese in 19th century Singapore. In P. G. L. Chew and A. Kramer-Dahl (eds.). *Reading Culture: Textual Practices in Singapore*, Times Academic Press, Singapore, 99–122.

Yap, E. X. Y. 2013. The transnational assembling of Marina Bay, Singapore. *Singapore Journal of Tropical Geography* 34(3): 390–406.

Yea, S. 2017. The art of not being caught: Temporal strategies for disciplining unfree labour in Singapore's contract migration. *Geoforum* 78(1): 179–188.

Yea, S. 2015. Trafficked enough? Missing bodies, migrant labour exploitation, and the classification of trafficking victims in Singapore. *Antipode* 47(4): 1080–1100.

Yeoh, B. S. A. 2006. Bifurcated labour: The unequal incorporation of transmigrants in Singapore. *Tijdschrift voor Economische en Sociale Geografie* 97(1): 26–37.

Yeoh, B. S. A. 1999. Global/globalizing cities. *Progress in Human Geography* 23(4): 607–616.

Yeoh, B. S. A. 1996. *Contesting Space: Power Relations and the Urban Built Environment in Colonial Singapore*. Oxford University Press, New York.

Yeoh, B. S. A., and T. C. Chang. 2001. Globalising Singapore: Debating transnational flows in the city. *Urban Studies* 38(7): 1025–1044.

Yeoh, B. S. A., and S. Huang. 2010. Sexualised politics of proximities among female transnational migrants in Singapore. *Population, Space and Place* 16(1): 37–49.

Yeoh, B. S. A., and K. Willis. 2005. Singaporeans in China: Transnational women elites and the negotiation of gendered identities. *Geoforum* 36(2): 211–222.

Yue, A. 2012. Queer Singapore: A critical introduction. In A. Yue and J. Zubillaga-Pow (eds.). *Queer Singapore: Illiberal Citizenship and Mediated Cultures*. Hong Kong University Press, Hong Kong, 1–25.

Yue, A. 2007. Creative queer Singapore: The illiberal pragmatics of cultural production. *Gay and Lesbian Issues and Psychology Review* 3(3): 149–160.

Yue, A., and J. Zubillaga-Pow (eds.). 2012. *Queer Singapore: Illiberal Citizenship and Mediated Cultures*. Hong Kong University Press, Hong Kong.

Zhang, J. 2012. From Hong Kong's capitalist fundamentals to Singapore's authoritarian governance: The policy mobility of neoliberalising Shenzhen, China. *Urban Studies* 49(13): 2853–2871.

Zhang, J., M. C.-W. Wu, and Brenda S. A. Yeoh. 2015. Cross-border marriage, transgovernmental friction, and waiting. *Environment and Planning D: Society and Space* 33(2): 229–246.

ARCHIVAL SOURCES

Department of Social Welfare. 1950. *Annual Report*. Department of Social Welfare, Singapore.

Department of Social Welfare. 1947. *A Social Survey of Singapore: A Preliminary Study of Some Aspects of Social Conditions in the Municipal Area of Singapore*. Government Printing Office, Singapore.

Department of Statistics. 1970. *Report on the Census of Population 1970*. Government Printer, Singapore.

Department of Statistics. 1957. *Report on the Census of Population 1957*. Government Printer, Singapore.

Goh Keng Swee. 1956. *Urban Incomes and Housing: A Report on the Social Survey of Singapore, 1953–54*. Department of Social Welfare, Singapore.

Housing Development Board. 1979. "I do"—the later the better. April 2–4.

Housing Development Board. 1976a. The guidance clinic. *Our Home*, February 4.

Housing Development Board. 1976b. Happy families. *Our Home*, April 14.

Housing Development Board. 1972a. Thinking of buying a HDB flat. *Our Home*.

Housing Development Board. 1972b. What family planning can do. *Our Home*. October 23–24.

Kaye, Barrington. 1960. *Upper Nankin Street, Singapore: A Sociological Study of Chinese Households Living in a Densely Populated Area*. University of Malaya Press, Singapore.

Khoo Hooi Leong v. Khoo Chong Yeok. 1930. *Straits Settlements Law Reports*. Government Printing Office, Singapore, 127–128.

Nathan, J. E. 1922. *The Census of British Malaya 1921*. Dunstable & Watford, London.

National Archives of Singapore, HB 778/47/2, Singapore Improvement Trust Housing Register Information Quiz.

National Archives of Singapore, HB 778/47/2, J. C. Lee, Estates Manager, Authorised occupation of Trust Flats, Appendix A.

National Archives of Singapore, HB 778/47/III, HDB Press Statement, August 4, 1967.

Report of the Chinese Marriage Committee. 1926. Government Printing Office, Singapore.

Simpson, W. J. 1907. *Report on the Sanitary Conditions of Singapore, 1901–1906.* Government Printing Office, Singapore.

Singapore. 1965. *White Paper on Family Planning in Singapore.* Government Printer, Singapore.

Singapore. 1955a. *Master Plan: Report of Survey.* Government Printing Office, Singapore.

Singapore. 1955b. Report of the Population Study Group. In *Master Plan: Reports of Study Groups and Working Parties.* Government Printing Office, Singapore.

Singapore. 1918. *Proceedings and Report of the Commission Appointed to Inquire into the Cause of the Present Housing Difficulties in Singapore and the Steps Which Should Be Taken to Remedy Such Difficulties.* Government Printing Office, Singapore.

Song Ong Siang. 1897. The position of Chinese women. *Straits Chinese Magazine* 1: 16–23.

Straits Settlements. 1938a. *Annual Report.* Government Printing Office, Singapore.

Straits Settlements. 1938b. *Proceedings of the Legislative Council of the Straits Settlements.* Government Printing Office, Singapore.

Straits Settlements. 1937. *Annual Report.* Government Printing Office, Singapore.

Straits Settlements. 1936. *Annual Report.* Government Printing Office, Singapore.

Straits Settlements. 1933. *Proceedings of the Legislative Council of the Straits Settlements.* Government Printing Office, Singapore.

Straits Settlements. 1927. *Proceedings of the Legislative Council of the Straits Settlements.* Government Printing Office, Singapore.

Straits Settlements. 1924. *Annual Department Reports.* Government Printing Office, Singapore.

Straits Settlements. 1923. *Report of the Venereal Diseases Committee.* Government Printing Office, Singapore.

Straits Settlements. 1921. *Proceedings of the Legislative Council of the Straits Settlements.* Government Printing Office, Singapore.

Straits Settlements. 1915. *Proceedings of the Legislative Council of the Straits Settlements.* Government Printing Office, Singapore.

Straits Settlements. 1905. *Annual Report.* Singapore: Government Printing Office.

Straits Settlements. 1900. *Annual Report.* Singapore: Government Printing Office.

UK National Archives, CO 659/13. Letter from Government House, Singapore to Colonial Office, November 14, 1939.

UK National Archives, CO 564/1. *First Report of the Advisory Committee on Social Hygiene,* August 1925.

INDEX

GEOGRAPHIES OF JUSTICE AND SOCIAL TRANSFORMATION

9 780820 355023